Text Generation

Writing 11 to 14

Book 2

Gregory and Hills

OXFORD
UNIVERSITY PRESS

OXFORD
UNIVERSITY PRESS

Great Clarendon Street, Oxford OX2 6DP

Oxford University Press is a department of the University of Oxford.
It furthers the University's objective of excellence in research,
scholarship, and education by publishing worldwide in

Oxford New York

Auckland Bangkok Buenos Aires Cape Town Chennai
Dar es Salaam Delhi Hong Kong Istanbul Karachi Kolkata
Kuala Lumpur Madrid Melbourne Mexico City Mumbai
Nairobi São Paulo Shanghai Taipei Tokyo Toronto

Oxford is a registered trade mark of Oxford University Press
in the UK and in certain other countries

British Library Cataloguing in Publication Data

Data available

ISBN 0 19 832070 1

10 9 8 7 6 5 4 3 2 1

Printed in Italy by Rotolito Lombarda.

Acknowledgements

We are grateful for permission to reproduce the following copyright
material:

BBC: extracts from www.bbc.co.uk/health, article by Dr Trisha McNair on
eating before exercise, article by Fiona Hayes on running, reprinted by
permission of the BBC; extracts from BBC News Online, bbc.co.uk/news,
Steve Schiffers 'Who gains from immigration?' 17.6.02; 'Should there be a
six-term school year?'; 'Prince battles video games' and responses by Anne
Fine, Mike Rawlinson, David Wilson, Steven Poole and George Grey
11.7.01; 'Video Games: Cause for Concern' 26.11.00 with quotes by Bunny
Martin and Dr Mark Griffiths; mobile phone article with quotes by
Professor William McNee 6.10.00; all reprinted by permission of the
contributors and the BBC.

John Bird and John Fortune: extract from *Bremner, Bird and Fortune*
produced by Vera Productions Limited for Channel 4, 2.3.03, reprinted by
permission of Vera Productions Limited.

British Nutrition Foundation: 'Cook-Chill Chain' poster, extracts
reprinted by permission of the British Nutrition Foundation.

Gillian Cross: review of *Caught in the Crossfire* by Alan Gibbons, copyright
© Gillian Cross 2003, from *The Guardian*, 12.4.03, reprinted by permission
of Guardian Newspapers Ltd.

Anne Fine BBC Online interview, reprinted by permission of the BBC and
David Higham Associates.

Adele Geras: review of *Inventing Elliott* by Graham Gardner, copyright ©
Adele Geras 2003, from *The Guardian*, 15.3.03, reprinted by permission of
Guardian Newspapers Ltd.

Fiona Hayes: extract from article on www.bbc.co.uk/health, reprinted by
permission of the BBC.

Julie Hearn: from *Follow Me Down* (OUP, 2003) copyright © Julie Hearn
2003, reprinted by permission of Oxford University Press.

The Independent: extracts from 'Soft, caring – and marketable. A new
breed of hero for today', *The Independent*, 8.2.98, copyright © Independent
Newspapers (UK) Ltd 1998, reprinted by permission of Independent
Newspapers (UK) Ltd.

Boris Johnson: extract from 'They're bleeding us dry to buy mountains of
red tape', *Daily Telegraph*, 27.2 03, reprinted by permission of the author
and The Telegraph Group.

Ellen MacArthur: accounts from www.ellenmacarthur.com published in
The Times, 15.2.03 and 25.2.03, reprinted by permission of Offshore
Challenges.

John McCarthy and Jill Morrell: *Some Other Rainbow* (Corgi, 1994),
reprinted by permission of Transworld Publishers, a division of The
Random House Group Ltd.

Geraldine MacCaughrean: extract from 'Perseus' in *The New Windmill
Book of Greek Myths*, reprinted by permission of David Higham Associates.

Dr Trisha McNair: extract from article on www.bbc.co.uk/health,
reprinted by permission of the BBC.

Emma Miller: from 'Barcelona; A mugger's paradise', *The Times*, 14.4.01,
copyright © NISyndication, London, 2001, reprinted by permission of News
International Newspapers Ltd.

Lilian Moore: 'Until I Saw the Sea' from *I Feel the Same Way*, copyright ©
Lilian Moore 1967, reprinted by permission of Marian Reiner for the
author.

Edwin Morgan: 'Glasgow Sonnet' from *Collected Poems* (1990), reprinted by
permission of the publishers, Carcanet Press Ltd.

The Newspaper: 'What's it all about', October 2001, reprinted by
permission of Young Media Group.

Grace Nichols: from *Whole of a Morning Sky* (Virago, 1986), copyright ©
Grace Nichols 1986, and lines from 'Sea Timeless Song' from *The Fat Black
Woman's Poems* (Virago, 1984), copyright © Grace Nichols 1984, reprinted by
permission of Curtis Brown Ltd, London on behalf of Grace Nichols.

NSPCC: extract from www.nspcc.org.uk web site, reprinted by permission
of the NSPCC.

Frank O'Connor: extract from *My Oedipus Complex and Other Stories*
(Penguin, 1963), copyright © Frank O'Connor 1963, reprinted by
permission of PFD on behalf of The Estate of Frank O'Connor.

Orion Publishing Group: book cover images of *Caught in the Crossfire* by
Alan Gibbons (Orion Children's Books, 2003) and *Inventing Elliot* by Graham
Gardner (Orion Children's Books, 2003).

Ovid: extract from 'Perseus' translated by Mary M Innes from *The
Metamorphoses* (Penguin Classics, 1955), copyright © Mary M Innes 1955,
reprinted by permission of Penguin Books Ltd.

James Reeves: 'The Sea' from *Complete Poems for Children* (Classic
Mammoth, 1994), copyright © James Reeves, reprinted by permission of
the James Reeves Estate, c/o Laura Cecil Literary Agency.

RSPCA: information leaflet 'Frogs and Toads: the facts' (1996), reproduced
by permission of the RSPCA.

Owen Sheers: lines from 'Sea Reading' from *The Blue Book* (Seren, 2000),
reprinted by permission of the publishers, Poetry Wales Press Ltd.

Steve Schiffers: 'Who gains from immigration?', BBC News Online,
bbc.co.uk/news 17.6.02, reprinted by permission of the BBC.

Meera Syal: extract from *Anita and Me* (Flamingo, 1996), copyright ©
Meera Syal 1996, reprinted by permission of HarperCollins Publishers Ltd.

R S Thomas: 'The Sea' from *Collected Poems 1945-1990* (J M Dent, 1993),
reprinted by permission of The Orion Publishing Group Ltd.

Sue Townsend: extract from *The Secret Diary of Adrian Mole aged 13³⁄₄*
(Methuen, 1982), reprinted by permission of The Random House Group Ltd.

Tim Utton: 'Using a mobile gives driver "tunnel vision"', *Daily Mail*,
30.1.03, reprinted by permission of Atlantic Syndication.

Keith Waterhouse: from 'Shelf-Room for Reading' in *Sharon and Tracy and
the Rest: The Best of Keith Waterhouse in the Daily Mail* (Hodder & Stoughton,
1992), reprinted by permission of David Higham Associates.

Wirral Learning Grid: exam revision advice from www.wirral-mbc.gov.uk
website, reprinted by permission of the Metropolitan Borough of Wirral.

Young Writer: extract from interview with Roger McGough, *Young Writer*
Issue 8, reprinted by permission of *Young Writer*.

We regret we have been unable to trace and contact all copyright holders
of material included before publication. If notified the publisher
undertakes to rectify any errors or omissions at the earliest opportunity.

The Publisher would like to thank the following for permission to
reproduce photographs:

Bridgeman Art Library: p 27; Corbis/Archivo Iconografico: p 49;
Corbis/Stephen Dupont: p 75; Corbis/Oen Franken: p 86 (middle and
bottom); Corbis/Franz-Marc Frei: p 86 (top); Corbis/Chris Hellier: p 48;
Corbis/Massimo Listri: p 47 Corbis/Amos Nachoum: p 29 (bottom); Corbis
Sygma: p 83; Corbis Sygma/Bernard Bisson: p 76; Corbis Sygma/Stephane
Cardinale: p 44 (left); Corbis Sygma/Stephane Ruet: p 44 (right); Corbis/Ed
Young: p 87; Corel Professional Photos: pp 14, 28, 29 (top), 30 (both), 60,
74, 57, 64; Sarah Darby: pp 26 (bottom right), 30 (bottom right); Digital
Vision: pp 56, 57, 61; Ronald Grant Archive: p 45; Hulton Archive: p 106;
Illustrated London News: p 39; Image Bank/Getty Images: p 26 (bottom
left); Image Source: pp 81, 88; Photodisc: pp 84, 121, 129; Rex
Features/Ken McKay: p 37; Rex Features/Ben Smith: pp 54, 80; Rex
Features/Team Kingfisher: p 82, Taxi/Getty Images: (cover and title page).

Illustration on p 17 is by Brien Pedley.

Special thanks go to the Real Writers:
Sue Mayfield, Julie Hearn, Helena Pielichaty, Tim Stimpson, John Hegley,
Andrew Solway, Tom Parkinson, Şenay Camgöz, Yehuda Sinai, Jane
Ramsey, Naomi Bracegirdle, Dan Curley
and to:
Lonely Planet Publications Ltd., The National Autistic Society, Oxfam, The
Official Playstation Magazine.

Text Generation

Writing 11 to 14

Contents

Contents

Who needs writers?

The modern world needs more writers than ever before. As you will see in the Real Writer sections of this book, many people make their living by writing for all sorts of purposes and audiences. They write advice; they write poetry; they inform us in books, magazines and travel guides; they give us information on web sites; they write speeches and scripts for radio programmes; they publish stories to entertain and challenge us; they write to persuade, to explain and to amuse us.

Why do I need writing skills?

Writing skills are vital if you want to communicate your thoughts and ideas to people further than you can shout! As an adult, you will find being able to write clearly and effectively will give you more power to express yourself and to persuade other people to see your viewpoint. As a student, writing skills will help you to achieve your potential in many subjects, not just in English. Being able to describe, analyse and present information is important across the curriculum, for example in Geography, History, Design and Technology and Science. Without writing skills, your 'voice' will be very quiet and limited to just the people who can hear you.

How will this book help?

Each unit in this book explores a different type of writing, e.g. writing to inform or writing to persuade. For each type of writing, you need to learn certain skills. The units are designed to help you to identify the key features of the different types of writing. Short writing tasks will help you to practise different skills as you work through the units. By the end of each unit you should feel confident enough to write your own complete text of that type.

Introduction

What's in each unit?

This is what you'll find in each unit:

A Real Writer – someone who uses writing skills in their work

Objectives – these are the skills that the unit will teach you

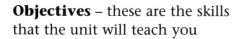

Objectives

In this unit you will learn how to:
- ✪ give written advice which offers alternatives and takes account of the possible consequences, e.g. money management for young people.

Introduction – this tells you about the type of writing you are going to explore

Introduction

This unit looks at . . .

Real texts – to give you models of top quality writing

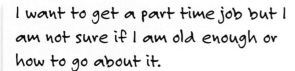

I want to get a part time job but I am not sure if I am old enough or how to go about it.

Activities – to help you explore the skills used for different types of writing

Checklists – to remind you of key features of different types of writing

Writing tasks – long and short tasks, similar to the ones in your Key Stage 2 tests, and which you will have again in tests during and at the end of Key Stage 3

Lots of activities – to do with a partner or in a small group

Arrows – to guide you through the writing process

Introduction

I don't like writing!

Some students find writing difficult and don't enjoy it. However, in this book we have tried to make writing easy, showing you how to build up your ideas, step by step, and then plan, draft and revise your work.

We have also tried to make this book fun, with lots of work in pairs or small groups, so you can exchange ideas and help each other. We've also tried to include interesting topics, such as the Internet, computer games, sport and chocolate!

It's easy to get disheartened as a writer, when you feel that what you write isn't good enough. But, as all the Real Writers will tell you, most of the best writing comes after lots of redrafting. Having someone to discuss your ideas with, and to give an opinion on your drafts, is very important. It is also good to think and talk about your own and other students' work. The more skilled you become at reading and judging others' writing, the better a writer you will become yourself.

Get ready to write!

Good writers must be willing to experiment and take risks, but they also need to know how texts work – this book will give you that knowledge. So, pick up your pen or pull out your keyboard and get ready to write. It's not always easy, but it should be fun and can be very rewarding. Happy writing!

Frances Gregory   Jacquie Hills

Real Writer: Sue Mayfield

Hi! I'm Sue Mayfield, and I write fiction for teenagers. Most of my books so far have been what you might call 'Contemporary Realism' – they're stories about young people in real-life, present-day situations, often grappling with difficult problems like bullying, family breakdown or bereavement.

For me, writing fiction is a bit like role-play or acting. It's about getting inside someone else's head and exploring how they would think or act or speak. I often write in the first person, which is a bit like putting on someone else's skin. My book *Reckless* is about twins Josh and Rachel, so I wrote some chapters from Rachel's point of view and some from Josh's. This enabled me to view and describe the same incidents from two perspectives and it also (I hope!) makes the reader feel he or she knows both characters quite personally.

Most of *Blue* – which is about a girl called Anna who is being subtly bullied – is told in the first person by Anna's friend Melanie. Then there are extracts from Anna's diary, which enable me to give Anna a 'voice' even though she is in a coma throughout the book. Thirdly there are short bursts of third-person present-tense narrative. These record things happening to Anna in the present (mostly unpleasant medical things!) a bit like a rolling CCTV camera, so I've tried to make these sections as clinical and impersonal as possible. The three different types of narrative are printed in three different fonts to make it clear who is 'speaking'.

Voices, my most recent book, has four different narrators. It's about sixth-formers doing a play, so it's laid out like a playscript – each section of text is like a character's lines. Instead of being called 'Chapter One', the first chapter is entitled 'Act One Scene One'.

Writing a book can be a great adventure. My advice to young writers is:
★ write about things you feel strongly about
★ keep a notebook to jot down interesting words you hear or descriptions of funny/beautiful/strange things you see
★ experiment with different points of view
★ be prepared to draft and redraft and redraft again – like polishing something until it really shines!

Objectives

In this unit you will learn how to:
- ✪ develop the use of commentary and description in narrative
- ✪ recognize some of the differences in sentence structure, vocabulary and tone between a modern English text and a text from another historical period.

Introduction

Think back to a story you have written. Did you try to guide the reader through the story? Did you try to build a relationship with your reader?

In this unit you'll develop your skills in engaging a reader. You'll learn how to make the most of narrative commentary and description and explore story-telling devices, some modern and some classical, as well as looking at how the English language has changed over time and across cultures.

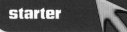

Starter activity

In pairs, brainstorm some examples of first, second and third person narratives you have encountered. Be prepared to share your findings.

Remember!

- ✪ <u>First person narratives use</u> 'I', e.g. 'I was walking down the road when …'
- ✪ <u>Second person narratives</u> use 'you', e.g. 'You are lying on a beach and …'
- ✪ <u>Third person narratives use</u> 'he/she/it/they', e.g. 'He ran towards her …'

Activities

1 Working with a partner, read the following extracts. Look at the pronouns and decide:
- ★ whether each extract is being told as a first or third person narrative
- ★ which extracts use the second person (directly address the reader).

Be ready to share your answers with the rest of the class.

A He didn't see her; but he heard her voice …

B In Darkville, you see, Jack Shakespeare thought he owned more than the mines and buildings …

C I was rapt. It was the best day of my life. I had asked Fiona to go with me and she'd said yes …

D They used John's dental records to identify the body, and afterwards they cremated it ...

H You don't know about me, without you have read a book by the name of 'The Adventures of Tom Sawyer', but that ain't no matter ...

E Well, what are you waiting for? Stretch your legs, go ahead and put your feet on a cushion, on two cushions ...

I The Junker Brothers had done a lot of bad things in their lives, but bank robbery was not one of them ...

F On 24 May 1863, which was a Sunday, my uncle, Professor Lidenbrock, came rushing back towards his little house, No.19 Konigstrasse, one of the oldest streets in the old quarter of Hamburg ...

J My sister, Mrs Joe Gargery, was more than twenty years older than I ...

G The planet Mars, I scarcely need remind the reader, revolves about the sun at a mean distance of 140,000,000 miles ...

write

2 Choose two of the extracts in the activity above, then add a few more sentences to your chosen extracts, using the same pronoun and narrative perspective.

discuss

3 Now rewrite your extracts, changing the pronouns to produce a different narrative perspective. Share your work with the class.

4 Was it easy to change the pronoun and narrative perspective?

5 What difference do you think this change might make to the way a reader responds to the story?

6 What advantages do you have when you write in the first person, and what disadvantages? Think of stories that you have read.

7 What advantages do you have when you write in the third person, and what disadvantages? Think of stories that you have read.

8 How easily could you tell a story in the second person? What is the point of directly addressing your reader when you are writing a story?

Describing the view

Read the extract from Meera Syal's autobiographical novel, *Anita and Me*. In this episode Meera's father thinks she has lied to him about some sweets. He is marching her to the sweet shop to check her story. The journey provides the ideal opportunity for Meera Syal to give the reader a glimpse of the neighbourhood in which she lives. On your first reading, notice how the writer engages the reader through vivid description.

read

Glossary

burnished –
polished
mercurial –
a reference to the
god Mercury,
who had wings
on his ankles
because he was
messenger of
the gods

> From the crest of the hill, on a clear day, you could see the industrial chimneys of Wolverhampton, smoking like fat men's cigars, and sometimes glimpse the dark fringes of Cannock Chase … But the horizon gradually disappeared as we marched down the hill towards Mr Ormerod's shop … There was my home, halfway down the hill, standing on the corner of the crossroads, one of the miners' tithe cottages huddled around a dirt yard which was the unofficial meeting place for our small community. There was the small overgrown park next to the yard, where the swings and rickety slide were watched over by the witch's hat of an ancient metal roundabout.
>
> I could see children riding their bikes, screeching in and around the parked cars and lines of washing, practising noisy manoeuvres which threw up clouds of dust, punctuating each skid like exclamation marks. I could see my mother, even at this distance, her brown skin glowed like a burnished planet drifting amongst the off-white bedsheets of her neighbours. She was wearing one of her slop-around outfits, a faded Punjabi suit whose billowing trousers rippled in the breeze, mercurial wings fluttering at her ankles.

Activities

1 Read the extract for a second time. This time, as you read, make a rough sketch or diagram of the scene described. When you have finished, think about what helped you to decide what to draw.

discuss

2 With a partner or in a small group, compare your sketches. Think about:
   ★ why you sketched what you did and how it relates to the extract
   ★ how Meera Syal's description helped you
   ★ which features of Syal's language helped form pictures in your mind
   ★ whether the writer appealed to any other senses apart from sight.

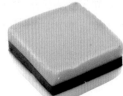

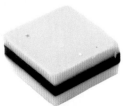

3 Does the writer like the place she describes? Think about:
★ what her feelings towards it are
★ which words tell you most about her feelings.

4 Find as many facts about Meera's mother in the extract as you can.

5 Which details in the extract might suggest the period of time in which this event occurs? Make a list.

6 How has Meera Syal engaged you in this description? Consider:
★ the order she writes in (identify the focus of each paragraph)
★ the use of simile and metaphor
★ the way the reader is guided about the scene (think about Syal's use of adverbials, e.g. 'From the crest…', 'halfway down…', etc.)
★ the narrative perspective.

Checklist

Begin a checklist of ways to describe a view. You may wish to use the list started for you below. How many features can you add?

Ways to describe a view

✪ Invite the reader to share the narrative viewpoint
✪ Use similes and metaphors to help the reader visualize the scene
✪ Include visual and aural detail – vivid adjectives, strong verbs – to add to the reader's imagination
✪ Use varied, detailed sentences to suggest the scene
✪ Guide the reader round the view – using adverbial phrases, for example
✪ Other …

Writing

Write a short paragraph describing the neighbourhood in which you live, using language to help your reader visualize or sense the place. Think about:
★ narrative perspective
★ your choice of verbs, nouns and adjectives
★ the use of complex sentences
★ the use of simile and metaphor
★ other ways of appealing to your reader's senses
★ key word choices to suggest your feelings about the place
★ a way of guiding your reader through or round the scene
★ ways of engaging the reader in the viewpoint.

Share your sentences with a partner. Together, think about:
★ which features of the writing you agree engage the reader
★ whether you can visualize each other's descriptions clearly
★ which features of a description are most important for a reader.

First person narratives

Jonathan Swift's *Gulliver's Travels* was published in 1726 and recounts the adventures of its fictional hero, Gulliver, in the first person. This extract describes Gulliver's first shipwreck. The first time you read the extract, note how little the English language has changed since 1726.

Glossary

Van Dieman's Land – the name for Tasmania, until 1855
computation - calculation
to abate – to become less intense
declivity – a downward slope
to conjecture – to form an opinion on the basis of incomplete information

It would not be proper for some reasons, to trouble the reader with the particulars of our adventures in those seas: let it suffice to inform him, that in our passage from thence to the East Indies, we were driven by a violent storm to the north-west of Van Diemen's Land. By an observation, we found ourselves in the latitude of 30 degrees 2 minutes south. Twelve of our crew were dead by immoderate labour, and ill food; the rest were in a very weak condition. On the fifth of November, which was the beginning of summer in those parts, the weather being very hazy, the seamen spied a rock, within half a cable's length of the ship; but the wind was so strong, that we were driven directly upon it, and immediately split. Six of the crew, of whom I was one, having let down the boat into the sea, made a shift to get clear of the ship, and the rock. We rowed by my computation, about three leagues, till we were able to work no longer, being already spent with labour while we were in the ship. We therefore trusted ourselves to the mercy of the waves; and in about half an hour the boat was overset by a sudden flurry from the north. What became of my companions in the boat, as well as of those escaped on the rock, or were left in the vessel, I cannot tell; but conclude they were all lost. For my own part, I swam as fortune directed me, and was pushed forward by wind and tide. I often let my legs drop, and could feel no bottom: but when I was almost gone, and able to struggle no longer, I found myself within my depth; and by this time the storm was much abated. The declivity was so small, that I walked nearly a mile before I got to the shore, which I conjectured was about eight o'clock in the evening. I then advanced forward near half a mile, but could not discover any sign of houses or inhabitants; at least I was in so weak a condition, that I did not observe them. I was extremely tired, and with that, and the heat of the weather, and about a half a pint of brandy that I drank as I left the ship, I found myself much inclined to sleep. I lay down on the grass, which was very short and soft; where I slept sounder than ever I remember to have done in my life, and as I reckoned, above nine hours; for when I awaked, it was just day-light. I attempted to rise, but was not able to stir: for as I happened to lie on my back, I found my arms and legs were strongly fastened on each side to the ground; and my hair, which was long and thick, tied down in the same manner.

think

discuss

Activities

1 Imagine that the narrative above was in the form of a cartoon strip. Sketch the six – very simple – illustrations you would include. Share your ideas with a partner and explain your choices to each other.

2 In pairs, write down three or four sentences (no more than 75 words) to summarize the sequence of events narrated in the Swift extract.

3 With another pair, discuss what you think will happen to Gulliver next. Which clues in the extract helped you to predict?

4 What is the narrative perspective in the Swift extract? How can you tell?

5 What challenges does the writing from 1726 present to you as a reader in the twenty-first century? Think about:
★ vocabulary and punctuation
★ sentence length and structure
★ details in the narrative.

6 List the techniques Swift uses to engage you as a reader.

Checklist

checklist

Below is a list of points to consider when using a fictional narrator. Refer back to the Swift extract and see how many points you can add.

Using a fictional narrator

- ✪ Use of a first person narrator to involve the reader
- ✪ Use of facts and figures to make the story sound real, not fictional
- ✪ The narrator addresses the reader directly, inviting a response
- ✪ No other character is mentioned by name so that the reader focuses on the first person narrator
- ✪ There is no dialogue, only the narrative commentary on events
- ✪ The pace is fast and the reader is not swamped with unnecessary detail
- ✪ Key vocabulary stresses the danger of the situation and builds tension
- ✪ Small details hint at events that will follow
- ✪ Other details are left unsaid to build the reader's curiosity
- ✪ Other points ...

Writing

Continue the Swift extract for another paragraph or so. Try to imitate Swift's style, using clues from the extract to decide what might happen next. (If you know the story, you do not need to follow what you know happens.)

You must engage your reader and try to keep up the relationship with the reader that Swift has begun. Do NOT introduce dialogue: you must continue to comment and describe. Remember to:

★ select appropriate techniques from the checklist above
★ employ the sort of vocabulary suitable for 1726 (use a dictionary and Swift's example) to guide your choices
★ experiment with sentence structures and lengths to match Swift's style. Read these aloud to a partner, to see if they sound right
★ think of appropriate historical detail (Gulliver says he has long hair, and his clothes will be typical of the early 1700s)
★ do some research: things people believed in the early eighteenth century might be less credible today.

1 Write a first draft. Keep in mind the style of Swift's original narrative.

2 Read your paragraph to a partner. Discuss these points:
★ Have you kept to the limited viewpoint of Gulliver himself?
★ What features have you used that your reader finds engaging?
★ What features of the eighteenth-century style have you used?
★ What additional feature could you have used to increase the sense of another age and to keep your reader's interest?

3 Prepare a final draft, taking any feedback into account.

4 Review what you have learnt about writing narrative commentary and description to engage your reader.

Third person narratives

Many writers tell their story as a third person narrative (rather than a first, like Swift). Third person narratives have their own advantages. The extract on the next page illustrates some of these.

read

Follow Me Down by Julie Hearn is set both in the present day and the eighteenth century and tells the story of a group of Londoners who try to save a friend's body from being used for entertainment.

In this extract, the Londoners are lurking in the graveyard where their friend has just been buried, ready to scare away the illegal grave robbers, who are led by Rafferty Spune. Tom – a boy from the twenty-first century – has dressed in a modern-day fluorescent skeleton suit to give the grave robbers the fright of their lives.

As you read, note the tension Hearn creates in order to engage her readers.

¹Tom listens.

²Nothing. Nothing except a faint rustling, over towards the cemetery gates, the kind of sound a small animal might make as it moves through grass, following a scent.

³But then ... Yes, Yes. There it is. Unmistakable this time. A low but insistent hooting; the kind of sound an owl might make – or a human being, as he spies, coming straight at him, the hulking shape of Rafferty Spune.

⁴No one speaks. It isn't allowed. Spune has been known to knock a fellow clean out, just for breathing too heavily while filling in a grave. Mattie Ladd, in particular, is being careful. Last dark night, in this very boneyard, he tripped over a tree root and went sprawling into a patch of nettles. A lesser man, he tells himself, would have screamed blue murder. For a tree root feels mighty like the clutch of a skeletal hand when you're tippy-toeing around folks' graves, at dead of night, without so much as a glow-worm lighting the way. And nettles hurt. They had hurt

him a lot. It is a matter of some pride to Mattie Ladd that he had picked himself up, without so much as a squeak, and done it so quick and quiet that Spune hadn't even noticed.

⁵Aha. They are approaching the exact same spot. He can tell. A few more steps and they'll be on it. Mattie Ladd hops a bit to the right, neatly avoiding the tree root. A little smirk lifts the scabby line of his mouth. He is learning. He is getting good. Very soon, he will be able to let go of the rope attached to the ginger man's belt – his only means, up to now, of tagging along, of keeping up with the others as they slink through inky darkness, avoiding the jut of crosses, the bruising points of angels' wings, by instinct.

⁶Soon, concludes Mattie Ladd … very soon, he will be striding through this grim, dark place as dauntless as Spune himself.

⁷He hears an owl, hoot close by. That's fine. He likes owls. It was rats you didn't want to come across in a boneyard. Them and ghosts …

think

Activities

1 You are going to film this scene for a TV version of the story.
   ★ You need to decide on the opening shot. From whose viewpoint must the camera be looking for the first three paragraphs?
   ★ For the next shot, does the camera stay in the same position? Use evidence from the text to support your answer.
   ★ What happens to the viewpoint in paragraph four? Think about which character might say 'For a tree root feels mighty like the clutch of a skeletal hand when you're tippy-toeing around folks' graves, at dead of night, without so much as a glow-worm lighting the way', and why the writer has included them here.
   ★ Why do you think the writer changes the viewpoint?

2 Answer these questions on the way in which Julie Hearn builds tension.
   ★ How does the writer build tension in the opening three paragraphs? Support your answer with evidence from the text.
   ★ Look at the verbs in the extract. Which tense are most of them in?
   ★ Where does the tense change and why?
   ★ How does the tension change once Rafferty Spune and his friends arrive?
   ★ How would you describe the pace of this piece of writing?
   ★ What do you think will happen next?
   ★ The reader of the story knows what should happen next, but the narrative remains engaging. How does Julie Hearn achieve this?

3 Consider the language used in the extract from *Follow Me Down*.
   ★ What features of the language make you suspect that, whilst the story may be set in the eighteenth century, it was not written in that period (look at vocabulary and sentence structure)?
   ★ What language features give the reader the sense that the event is set in the past?

write

Writing

Continue the extract from *Follow Me Down* for two or three paragraphs. In your first paragraph, the narrative must return to the limited viewpoint of Tom, but from your second paragraph onwards you can choose the viewpoint yourself (Rafferty Spune, for example). Remember that you are writing commentary, NOT dialogue. You must direct what the reader sees and feels as if you were a cameraman.

1 Write a rough first draft of your narrative.

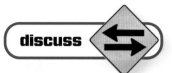

discuss

2 Discuss your writing with a partner.
★ Is the writing engaging?
★ Can you imagine the scene vividly – have you used sensory detail?
★ Does the change in viewpoint add to the reader's engagement?
★ What are your two favourite features?
★ How could you improve your narrative commentary?

3 Prepare a final draft, taking into account the feedback you have received. Remember to check spelling and punctuation.

checklist

Checklist

Begin a checklist of ways a writer can engage a reader. You might like to follow the example started for you below. How many features can you add?

Ways to engage a reader

⊗ Create tension through short sentences, repetition and changes in pace
⊗ Suggest movement and excitement in longer, more detailed sentences
⊗ Involve the reader in the characters' feelings or limited experiences by making them share the characters' viewpoints
⊗ Use the sort of language appropriate for your characters (particularly when describing their thoughts/viewpoint), but do not include any direct speech
⊗ Describe sensory detail that helps the reader visualize the scene
⊗ Give the reader hints of what is to follow
⊗ Create anticipation by switching viewpoints at key moments
⊗ Other features ...

Unit plenary

discuss

Discuss what your targets will be next time you have to write:
★ to engage your reader through narrative commentary or description
★ to imitate the style of another historical period.

Additional writing tasks

write

1 **Short writing task.** Write a third person account of a recent event from home or school, into which you introduce tension or a sense of anticipation. You may include more than one character's viewpoint, or address your reader directly.

2 **Longer writing task.** Imagine that Gulliver's travels extend to your school in the present time. Gulliver, all alone, walks up to the main entrance, past some of the school buildings, through the reception area and into the school hall, where an assembly is in progess. Using appropriate language and engaging detail, complete this episode as a piece of narrative commentary and description.

Real Writer: Julie Hearn

Figurative language ... aaaargh! Sometimes I wonder how I ever got my Masters Degree, or wrote my first novel, when the technical terms for the way language is used make me feel so nervous – I still get alliteration and assonance muddled up even now!

Having said that, there is nothing more satisfying, for a writer, than playing around with words until they say something original, in a pleasing way. It's like painting a picture or making a stew. Just about anyone can produce a drawing of a stick man, or slap a few onions in with some meat. But, in the same way that shading the picture or seasoning the stew adds subtlety and flavour to the creation, learning how to use language imaginatively (or figuratively) can make all the difference to a piece of writing.

I like to compare my own writing to painting (probably because I hate cooking!). The use of simile and metaphor, in particular, seem to me to work like light and shade, adding depth to characterization and making the whole story more satisfying. It takes practice, but once you've got the hang of using these techniques, you'll find it can really bring a narrative to life – which is what really draws the reader in!

I used to be a journalist, so I learned through trial and error to avoid 'purple prose', which is a trade term for over-exaggerated feelings and cringe-making clichés. I do love similes though, and try to push the limits of purple prose as far as possible without going over the top. My similes usually end up a kind of bright mauve!

If you're going to use figurative language, always make it earn its keep by telling the reader something new, or highly significant, about a person, place or situation. Don't just throw it in for the sake of it!
And a good thesaurus, by the way, is invaluable for finding exactly the right word when you're experimenting with figurative language. I wouldn't be without mine. It's my paintbox – figuratively speaking!

Follow Me Down
JULIE HEARN
'someone whose work I always read with pleasure'
Philip Pullman

Objectives

In this unit you will learn how to:
- ✪ appreciate the impact of figurative language in texts
- ✪ experiment with figurative language in conveying a sense of character and setting
- ✪ recognize how texts refer to and reflect the culture in which they were produced.

Introduction

As a writer you need to be able to engage a reader in your narrative – if there is nothing to interest the reader, he or she is unlikely to read on! So how are you going to keep the reader's attention?

This unit focuses on how particular figures of speech can be used to communicate a more vivid and powerful sense of character and setting. You will also explore how a writer can create a specific mood or atmosphere, as well as beginning to think about how a writer sets about establishing a sense of time, place and culture in his or her writing.

Starter activity

As a class, brainstorm as many features of figurative language as you can remember, e.g. simile, metaphor, etc. Then, in pairs, think of and note down one example for each feature. Share your examples with the class.

Activity

Carefully read the short extracts below and on page 23, all of which are taken from the novels of Charles Dickens. In pairs, link each extract to one or more of these most common features of figurative language:
- ★ metaphor
- ★ onomatopoeia
- ★ assonance
- ★ simile
- ★ alliteration
- ★ repetition
- ★ personification.

A The rusty old gentleman

B Carpets rolled into great scrolls

C Her light came along the dark passage like a star

D Everything else seemed stranded and still

E He had long iron grey hair

F   There was a rattling and a trembling all day long

H   Tall chimneys out of which serpents of smoke trailed

G   It was a town of unnatural red and black like the painted face of a savage

I   People who went in and out at the same time, with the same sound upon the same pavements to do the same work

J   The rain is ever falling, drip, drip, drip

Character and setting

read

Read this extract from *Follow Me Down* by Julie Hearn. The novel is about Tom, a twelve-year-old who finds himself able to travel back in time to the eighteenth century. He has done this once before, when he was only two years old. Here he is reunited with an old acquaintance. On your first reading notice how the writer engages you in the character of Astra.

JULIE HEARN

'someone whose work I always read with pleasure'
Philip Pullman

It was still his grandmother's basement and yet it wasn't. The commotion out on the street was all wrong for a start: a clattering – wheels, hooves, clogs, Tom couldn't tell – and the kind of raucous shouting and carrying on that, ordinarily, would have lost the Black Raven its licence. The basement window had been blocked up with planks and old sacking so that not a chink or a spyhole remained ...

There was a rustling in the far corner, then a small sigh. An exquisite little face appeared in the glow of a newly-lit candle and regarded Tom, forlornly. He went forward then, just a little way, blinking back the tears that threatened, suddenly, to embarrass him.

'Hello, Astra.' Should he hug her or shake her tiny hand? Both gestures, he realised, might easily snap her bones; yet the moment demanded something more than words, so overwhelmed was he to have found, once again, this being who had always been with him, he realised that now, hovering lightly on the edges of his dreams.

'Astra?' Her voice was shrill, her face mewling, like a kitten's. 'Is that who I am then? Is that what I told yer last time? Well Astra ... Fairyspawn ... the Princess of blessed Kolozsvar – it don't matter no more. You can push off. Go on. You're a grow'd man now and grow'd men ain't never done me no kindness.'

She jammed her candle into a rusty sconce, jutting from the wall, threw herself face down onto a nasty-looking pile of rags and straw, and burst into sobs as acute as the flailing of windchimes. 'You was such a dear little mannikin,' she hiccupped. 'Now look at yer.'

Tom stepped closer ...

He was so near to her now that he could see bits of muck caught in the thistledown of her hair. Her spine was juddering like a clothes line beneath the filthy shift she wore. The soles of her feet looked too small to walk on. But for the trembling, and the crying, she could have been a doll; an unwanted doll tossed on a rubbish heap.

Glossary

raucous – a disturbingly harsh and loud noise
sconce – a candle holder that is attached to a wall
acute – high, shrill
to judder – to shake or vibrate rapidly and powerfully

Activities

think

1 What impression do you get of Astra from the physical description of her in this extract? Think about:
   ★ the use of adjectives and adverbs
   ★ the use of verbs
   ★ references to her physical size
   ★ references to dirt/grime.

2 How does Astra's speech add to the effect of her physical appearance? Think about:
   ★ what she says
   ★ how she says it.

3 How does the writer engage the reader in this extract? Think about:
   ★ the description of the setting
   ★ which figures of speech help you to imagine the scene
   ★ which other words make the scene vivid
   ★ Astra's speech.

4 Which figures of speech contribute most to your picture of Astra? Do any other word choices contribute to this picture?

5 How do you think Tom feels about Astra? Think about:
   ★ which words tell you most about his feelings
   ★ whether the figures of speech suggest these feelings.

6 Can you guess anything about the historical period in which the text is set? Which details might help you to work this out?

7 In pairs, discuss the benefits of using figurative language to create character and setting in narrative. Think about what you have observed in Julie Hearn's writing.

Checklist

Look through this checklist of advantages of using figurative language. Can you add more?

Advantages of figurative language

⭐ Helps the reader to visualize the place or the character or to hear sounds or contribute to other imagined sensations
⭐ Creates strong feelings in the reader, through association or imagination, which involves the reader in characters and events
⭐ Provides mood and atmosphere in the writing
⭐ Other advantages ...

REMEMBER!
If figures of speech do not make the writing more vivid or memorable, then it is best not to include them at all, or to change the particular technique used to one that works better.

Writing

Now try writing a short piece of narrative of your own, limiting the piece to two paragraphs only. Choose a place that you associate with someone you know quite well and concentrate on using figurative language to:
★ describe the place
★ describe the person.

Use figurative language to give vivid detail to engage your reader.

Share a draft version of your description with a partner and consider its strengths before redrafting for a final copy. Your task is to judge whether the figures of speech succeed in making the writing more vivid and memorable.

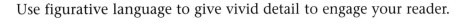

Mood and atmosphere

Starter activity

In a small group, brainstorm as many adjectives that can be used to describe mood and atmosphere as you can in five minutes.

In pairs, choose one word, then craft two or three sentences about an imaginary situation in which you create that mood or atmosphere, but without using the word itself. For example, if you walk into a room and everyone is very quiet but they look pale and worried, and are sitting on the edge of their seats, we might say the atmosphere is tense or expectant.

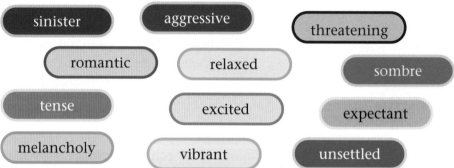

sinister aggressive threatening romantic relaxed sombre tense excited expectant melancholy vibrant unsettled

discuss

Share some of your sentences with the class. Did you use any features of language to create atmosphere and, if so, which? Has anyone used exaggerated language to achieve the desired effect, such as when we say 'there were millions of people at the party'? We call this figure of speech HYPERBOLE.

read

Now read the extract on page 27, taken from Charles Dickens' novel *Great Expectations*. The fictional narrator, Pip, is alone in his lodgings in London one evening. The weather has been very bad. As you read focus on identifying the mood or atmosphere that Dickens creates.

It was wretched weather; stormy and wet, stormy and wet; and mud, mud, mud, deep in all the streets. Day after day, a vast heavy veil had been driving over London from the East, and it drove still, as if in the East there were an Eternity of cloud and wind. So furious had been the gusts, that high buildings in town had had the lead stripped off their roofs; and in the country, trees had been torn up, and sails of windmills carried away; and gloomy accounts had come in from the coast, of shipwreck and death. Violent blasts of rain had accompanied these rages of wind, and the day just closed as I sat down to read had been the worst of all.

Alterations have been made in that part of the Temple since that time, and it is not now so lonely a character as it had then, nor is it so exposed to the river. We lived at the top of the last house, and the wind rushing up the river shook the house that night, like discharges of cannon, or breakings of a sea. When the rain came with it and dashed against the windows, I thought, raising my eyes to them as they rocked, that I might have fancied myself in a storm-beaten lighthouse. Occasionally, the smoke came rolling down the chimney as though it could not bear to go out into such a night; and when I set the doors open and looked down the staircase, the staircase lamps were blown out; and when I shaded my face with my hands and looked through the black windows (opening them ever so little was out of the question in the teeth of such wind and rain) I saw that the lamps in the court were blown out, and that the lamps on the bridges and the shore were shuddering, and that the coal fires in barges on the river were being carried away before the wind like red-hot splashes in the rain.

Activities

think

1 Which details give you some sense of the period in which this extract is set? Make a list.

2 What is Dickens describing in the first paragraph?

3 Find as many examples of figures of speech in the extract as you can. Think about:
   ★ how they help the reader to feel and see the scene vividly
   ★ Dickens' use of alliteration, repetition and other word choices.

4 Look at the way Dickens constructs his sentences. How does this, and the way they are connected, contribute to your sense of the scene?

5 What is Dickens describing in the second paragraph? Think about:
   ★ which figures of speech are most vivid for you here
   ★ which figures of speech helped you to imagine the scene, or to hear the sound of, and feel, the weather.

6 What mood and atmosphere does Dickens create here?

7 Which particular feature of the language do you find most effective? Give reasons for your choice.

Checklist

Have a look through the checklist below. Add your own features to the list.

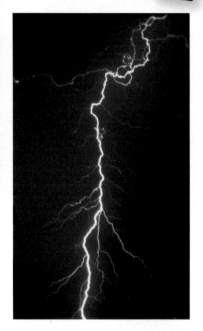

Ways of creating mood and atmosphere

✪ Appeal to the sense of sound through onomatopoeia
✪ Appeal to the sense of sight through similes and metaphors
✪ Make an idea more vivid through hyperbole
✪ Appeal to the readers' feelings through the combination of the figures of speech
✪ Use a variety of sentence structures and lengths
✪ Use patterns in the sentences, e.g. repetition of words, phrases or sentence structures, or balancing differences to create patterns and rhythms
✪ Other methods ...

Writing

Think of an occasion when you have experienced extreme weather conditions, then write a short description (no more than two paragraphs). Remember to:
★ use figurative language to make your writing vivid
★ make good use of repetition and, if you choose, hyperbole to create effects
★ make every word work overtime.

Look at your work with a partner and test how well you communicate with your reader by discussing:
★ which figures of speech you found most useful in your own writing and why
★ which figures of speech you chose to ignore and why.

Evoking place and culture

Read the following extract, taken from *Whole of a Morning Sky* by Grace Nichols. Focus on the way the writer not only creates mood and atmosphere through her use of figurative language, but also evokes a particular place and culture.

Georgetown. Magic in the street lights, money everywhere, people everywhere, walking up and down the pavements eating nuts, channa, ice-cream cones, popcorn. Flamboyant trees shedding red petals in the avenues. On Friday nights women selling gleaming coils of black pudding at the street corners in little carts.

Georgetown. Stabroek Market with the big clock. The dim crowded rumshops, ten alone you count on Camp Street, and the voices from them, not voices at all, but words, just words jumble up together.

You press your mother into letting you run every little errand just for the chance to walk down those streets.

You keep going to Norton – the one with the fountain. Not the side full of rusty cars, broken down houses and the funeral parlour, but the part with the blue and white café and the marble fountain, the water curving in an arc into the air, then falling like fine rain into a pool below.

On Sunday afternoons, you, Dinah, your mother and Anthony go down to the sea wall. Your mother played here as a girl, running around the sandy beach below, wading in the water, watching the waves bring in shoals of little four-eye fish and taking them back out again. One day, she and her cousin were playing on the beach. They could see the skies getting darker and knew a rainstorm was coming but still they stayed. It took the first peel of thunder to send them running home because it felt just as if the whole Atlantic was opening to swallow them up.

Activities

think

1 Brainstorm some immediate observations about this writing. Think about how it differs from the other texts you have read in this unit.

2 Which clues in the text might help the reader to locate the geographical setting and culture of the narrative? Make a list. Can you guess where this narrative is set? Think about:
   ★ vocabulary that is specific to the culture described, e.g. rum shops, the Atlantic, four-eyed fish, the trees with red petals, channa, etc.
   ★ the list of observations you have prepared in question 1.

4 The writer creates a variety of moods in the extract.
   ★ What are they?
   ★ How does Nichols use contrast to make these moods more evident?

5 Pick out some examples of figurative language Nichols uses to create the mood of the Caribbean.

6 What other techniques does the writer use to create mood? Consider the list below. Can you add more?
   ★ Incomplete sentences to stress the action; short, childlike sentences to suggest excitement
   ★ Lists to build detail and a sense of variety
   ★ Second person to invite the reader to share in the experience

★ Present tense and participles of the verb to stress action and motion
★ Change of tense at the end for a flashback
★ Contrast – seaside/city, rich/poor, crowded street/empty Atlantic, colours
★ Changes in mood as location varies
★ Appeals to sense of taste and sound as well as vision

 checklist

Checklist

Ways used to suggest a sense of place and culture

✪ Geographical references – names or features of landscape
✪ Biological references – animals, plants (e.g. four-eyed fish, trees with red petals)
✪ Cultural references – foods, clothes, habits, music (e.g. rum shops, selling black pudding on street corners)
✪ Special vocabulary used only in that region (e.g. channa)
✪ Culturally specific metaphors (e.g. white as snow)
✪ Use of dialect or culturally specific features of grammar
✪ Other features ...

 write

Writing

Write a third person narrative in which you describe a location, and in which you introduce a character that is typical of that location. (The location you choose could be anywhere in the world.) Use the checklists in this unit to help you. Remember to:

★ think carefully about setting and character – use figurative language to bring your narrative alive
★ build up the mood and atmosphere in your writing – think about the tense you are going to use, details to include, etc.

1 First, think of a location. Choose a place that is not already familiar to you – perhaps somewhere you would like to visit.

2 Next, do some research. Find out about the climate, the food, the people, the landscape, etc. of your chosen location. Your aim is to create not only a mood, but also a sense of place and culture.

3 Now think about a character. Who are they and what are they like? How do they speak and move?

4 Begin to write your description. Don't name your location immediately. Use your description to give clues to the reader.

discuss

5 Swap your work with a partner and see if you can:
★ identify the intended mood and atmosphere
★ identify the place and culture
★ identify two strengths in the writing and one aspect you could improve.

Unit plenary

discuss

Discuss:
★ what you have learnt about the ways in which figurative language can convey a sense of character, setting and mood
★ what impact your use of figures of speech had on the quality of your own writing
★ what you have learnt about the ways in which a sense of place and culture can be conveyed in a piece of narrative.

Additional writing tasks

write

1 **Short writing task.** Write the opening of a novel set in a particular city or location at a particular time. End the piece as you introduce a character into this setting.

2 **Longer writing task.** Write a first person narrative in which a character looks from a window on to a particular view. Use the description of the view to create the character's mood and the atmosphere of the piece.

Real Writer: Helena Pielichaty

Hi! I'm Helena Pielichaty and I write fiction for young adults. My books tend to focus on real life situations that take place in the present.

One of my mum's favourite moans to me when I was a teenager was, 'It's not what you say, it's the way that you say it', and I suppose that sums up 'tone' (not to mention my character!) in a nutshell!

Maybe I shouldn't tell you this, but I don't actually plan the tone in my stories in a conscious way. In fact, it often isn't until I read the work out loud that I realize the tone I have set. Stranger still is when the lilt of the dialogue and narrative leads me to read the story in a regional accent! One of my characters, Sammie Wesley, always makes me want to drop into 'Brummie' for some reason.

When I am writing in the first person, as the main character talking directly to the reader, I have to be careful with tone. I am forever 'toning down' or 'toning up'. For example, when I began writing *Starring Jolene*, one of the books in my *After School Club* series, I knew that Jolene was angry with the world and I wanted that to come across from the outset. My original opening paragraph read:

Don't read this if you're one of those people who thinks boys are 'cool' and kittens are 'sweet' and you wear lip gloss in flavours like pina colada and raspberry ripple. You're not my type. I'm not interested in you and I don't want you to be interested in me.

The tone of this was too alienating. Half my readers would have thought 'suit yourself' and closed the book, which is the last thing I wanted them to do, so I toned it down. The story now opens:

Before I start, if you're one of those people who thinks boys are 'cool' and kittens are 'sweet' and you have hundreds of lip glosses in different flavours like raspberry ripple and pina colada, I don't think you should read my story. You won't like it.

Can you hear the difference? Just by exchanging the word 'don't' (a direct order) to 'before I start' (more of a warning) I have softened the tone, if only slightly. Hearing the difference is the real key. My advice to anyone unsure about the tone of a text? Read it aloud!

Objectives

In this unit you will learn how to:

⭐ experiment with different language choices to imply meaning and to establish the tone of a piece, e.g. ironic, indignant

⭐ identify the ways implied and explicit meanings are conveyed in different texts, e.g. irony, satire.

Introduction

When you read a narrative text, do you hear the writer's voice as you read? How does the writer help you to read the text in the right way? How do you know what tone of voice to use when reading a text? Are there times when you are not sure? Do you sometimes pick up a tone in that voice that tells you not to take what is written at face value?

In this unit you will learn to recognize, master and experiment with subtle tones of voice. You will also learn how to inject your writing with humour, irony and satire.

Starter activity: The lowest form of wit

With a partner, look at the sentences below. How many different meanings can you give to each sentence simply by using different tones of voice?

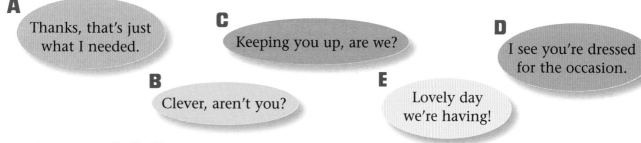

A Thanks, that's just what I needed.

B Clever, aren't you?

C Keeping you up, are we?

D I see you're dressed for the occasion.

E Lovely day we're having!

Activities

1 Look back at sentences A to E above. Which sentence has the most meanings depending on the tone of voice you used?

2 Once you have decided which is the most flexible sentence, put each meaning of that sentence into a suitable context. For example, one meaning of sentence A might be:

John was helping his Mum mend the car. He knew she needed the other toolbox and passed it to her. 'Thanks, that's just what I needed,' she said.

Another meaning might be:

John was helping his Mum mend the car. He wasn't watching where he was going and tripped over the oil can, spilling the oil everywhere. 'Thanks,' she said, 'that's just what I needed.'

3 Think about the activities above. Did you find a tone of voice that allowed you to say one thing and mean something else?

4 Read the following examples aloud and experiment with the tone of voice.

A A student is falling asleep while reading a book in class. The teacher says, 'Keeping you up, are we?'

B Mr Smith drives into Mr Jones's new car. Mr Jones climbs out of his car and says, 'Thanks, that's just what I needed!'

C Anne Robinson says to the weakest link, 'Clever, aren't you?'

5 Which one word would you use to describe the tone of voice in sentences A to C? Did you use this tone of voice in any of your answers to question 2?

These comments are **sarcastic**. We often use sarcasm in day to day life – it can be amusing to the person who uses it, but it usually makes fun of someone and can be unkind. In a sarcastic remark we mean the opposite of what is being said.

Some people claim that sarcasm is 'the lowest form of wit' because it isn't particularly clever and is usually used to hurt someone's feelings. However, thinking about sarcasm is a good starting point for discussing irony.

A writer who uses irony does not state things directly. Instead, he or she implies or suggests a meaning through the tone of voice used in the writing. The writer's tone of voice warns the reader to look beneath the surface meaning. Sometimes irony makes us laugh, but it can also make us think seriously about an issue.

6 Research the origin of the word 'irony'. This will help you to understand its basic meaning – 'irony' has a really interesting origin, too!

Irony and humour

read

Read the extracts below. What makes them amusing for a reader?

A In these short extracts from *The Secret Diary of Adrian Mole aged 13 ³/₄* Adrian comments on his mother's friendship with the next door neighbour.

> **Friday 16th January**
>
> Mr Lucas came round and offered to take my mother shopping in the car. They dropped me off at school. I was glad to get out of the car what with all the laughing and cigarette smoke. We saw Mrs Lucas on the way. She was carrying big bags of shopping. My mother waved, but Mrs Lucas couldn't wave back.
>
> **Wednesday 21st January**
>
> Mr and Mrs Lucas are getting a divorce! They are the first down our road. My mother went next door to comfort Mr Lucas. He must have been very upset because she was still there when my father came home from work.

B *My Oedipus Complex* by Frank O'Connor is narrated by an only child, Larry, whose father is away fighting in the First World War. Larry tells the reader about the family's preparations for Christmas.

> They discussed what Mother and I should do during the day, what Santa Claus should give a fellow for Christmas, and what steps should be taken to brighten the home. There was that matter of the baby, for instance. Mother and I could never agree about that. Ours was the only house in the terrace without a new baby, and Mother said we couldn't afford one till Father came back from the war because they cost seventeen and six. That showed how simple she was. The Geneys up the road had a baby, and everyone knew they couldn't afford seventeen and six. It was probably a cheap baby, and mother wanted something really good, but I felt she was too exclusive. The Geneys' baby would have done us fine.

Activities

1 What is the writer of extract A implying? Think about:
* ★ the surface meaning
* ★ what the tone of voice in this extract suggests.

2 What is the writer of extract B telling us about Larry? Think about:
* ★ how old Larry might be
* ★ how much/little Larry understands about the adult world
* ★ what Larry thinks of his mother's attitude about babies.

3 Would extract B be as humorous if, for example, Larry's mother had been telling us about Larry's ideas on babies? Why not?

4 Read each extract aloud. Find the tone of voice intended by each writer.

5 Which characteristics do the two pieces of writing share? Make a list.

Checklist

Begin a checklist of the ways in which an author can create an ironic tone of voice in a text. You may like to use the list below as a model.

Ways to create an ironic text

* ✪ Choose a first person fictional narrator
* ✪ Make the narrator innocent or ignorant of the facts that are revealed
* ✪ Exaggerate a young narrator's misunderstanding of the 'adult' world for comic effect
* ✪ The narrator uses colloquial (everyday, informal) language
* ✪ Share 'a joke' with the reader at the expense of a simple-minded, first-person narrator (this is an example of irony for comic effect)
* ✪ Suggest (indirectly, through tone of voice) problems in the adult world (a writer could use this device to make comments about people that appear to be innocent but are actually critical)
* ✪ Other features ...

Writing

Write a short piece of narrative in which you use an innocent or ignorant narrator for comic effect. If you wish, you could continue one of the extracts you have studied above. Try to:
* ★ follow the colloquial style of the extracts
* ★ amuse your reader by using an ignorant or an innocent voice.

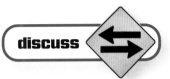

discuss

Read your narrative aloud to a partner. How successful is it? Was there anything you found particularly challenging about this task?

Satire and criticism

Have you noticed that television comics – especially those who work in pairs – use a similar technique to the writers featured above? One of the pair pretends to be ignorant, while the other acts the know-all to comic effect. Sometimes, the things comics say can be very critical of human actions. This is where humour and irony start to become SATIRE. The real joke is making fun of human failings such as stupidity, greed, pride or prejudice. Just think about how mimics like Alistair McGowan and Rory Bremner make fun of famous people.

In this example – taken from the television series 'Bremner, Bird and Fortune' – a mixture of humour and irony aims to expose human behaviour. Two characters from the planet Zog are discussing the reasons why Zog must attack the Earth. The supreme Arkon of Zog explains why he believes that weapons of mass destruction are being built in the now disused Millennium Dome. A monitor is showing pictures of various sites on Earth.

read

Read through this scene carefully twice.

JOHN BIRD: (the supreme Arkon or leader from the planet Zog)
Well of course we've known for some time that they've possessed old-fashioned conventional weapons. You see one being tested just now.
JOHN FORTUNE: (as an interviewer)
Oh yes. Yes indeed. But these are puny weapons aren't they? I mean they couldn't possibly reach us in any threatening sense.
JOHN BIRD:
No, no they only use them on each other. But our satellite reconnaissance, has shown something rather more sinister I'm afraid.
JOHN FORTUNE:
Really! That is disquieting. Oh!
JOHN BIRD:
And here it is you see. This is um, analysts have said this may well be a bitterly crude copy of one of our earlier military space vehicles, the Mark 1 Battle Saucer.
JOHN FORTUNE:
But surely that's a building that they put up to celebrate some sort of anniversary, didn't they?

> *JOHN BIRD*:
> Yes.
> *JOHN FORTUNE*:
> Wasn't that something called the dome?
> *JOHN BIRD*:
> Well that's I think what they'd like us to believe.
> *JOHN FORTUNE*:
> I see. But surely that's been abandoned and derelict for the last 3 years?
> *JOHN BIRD*:
> Yes. Again that may be a ruse. I think that, well I mean, looking at it realistically, no one would spend that amount of money or time to er, produce something they were just going to let rot, and not use you know. It's just beyond belief.

Activities

1 How does the irony work in this sketch? Identify:
  - ★ what the 'sinister' object is
  - ★ what Arkon believes the object is copied from
  - ★ what the Earthlings want everyone to believe
  - ★ why Arkon believes it must be a 'ruse'
  - ★ why this belief is ironic (i.e. the reality is the opposite of what he states).

2 Can you identify any other statements that are ironic?
  - ★ Look at the early comments about weapons.
  - ★ Explain how the irony works (i.e. the difference between what is stated and the reality).

Writing

1 In pairs, extend the 'Bremner, Bird and Fortune' script for a few more lines. Keep the tone of the original in mind as you write.

2 When you are happy with what you have produced, perform the sketch (and your extension) in front of the class.

3 After your performance, consider:
  - ★ whether your new lines worked
  - ★ what sort of voice used to make the scripts amusing
  - ★ how you could improve your extension of the sketch.

4 Draft a final version of your extension.

Satire and social change

Satirists make fun of people or organizations that they feel need to be criticized because they think that they are wrong or misguided. Satire aims to change the way people think or behave for the better. Like irony, satire relies upon the reader being intelligent enough to recognize that the writer doesn't mean what he or she says literally.

One technique used by satirists is irony. It is often used for comic effect, but the intentions behind it are frequently very serious, even if it still makes us laugh. For example, Charles Dickens was deeply concerned about many people who lived, worked and died young in the polluted industrial cities of England in the nineteenth century. He wrote the novel, *Hard Times*, to draw attention to their dreadful situation. Thanks to people like Dickens, factory laws were changed and people's lives improved.

Irony is one of the tools Dickens uses to criticize – or satirize – the wealthy and self-concerned mill-owners who profited while their workers suffered. As you read the following extract decide what Dickens is actually saying the mill-owners ought and need to do.

read

A sunny midsummer day. There was such a thing sometimes, even in Coketown.

Seen from a distance in such weather, Coketown lay shrouded in a haze of its own, which appeared impervious to the sun's rays. You only knew the town was there, because you knew there could have been no such sulky blotch upon the prospect without a town …

The wonder was, it was there at all. It had been ruined so often, that it was amazing how it had borne so many shocks. Surely there never was such a fragile china-ware as that which the millers of Coketown were made. Handle them never so lightly, and they fell to pieces with such ease that you might suspect them of having been flawed before. They were ruined, when they were required to send labouring children to school; they were ruined, when inspectors were appointed to look into their works; they were ruined when such inspectors considered it doubtful whether they were quite justified in chopping people up with machinery; they were utterly undone, when it was hinted that perhaps they need not always make quite so much smoke.

think

Activities

1 Read the extract aloud. Think about:
- ★ what tone of voice you need to use to make it sound right
- ★ which words you need to emphasize to gain the right effect.

2 Why do you think Dickens chose the name 'Coketown' for his fictional city? (Looking up the definition of 'coke' will help.)

3 What does the opening paragraph suggest about Coketown? How does Dickens make this suggestion?

4 What do the words 'shrouded' and 'sulky blotch' in the second paragraph imply about Coketown?

5 What is Dickens really saying in the third paragraph? Does he mean exactly what he says, or is he using irony? Justify your answers.
- ★ Does he really believe the mill-owners to be as 'fragile' as fine china?
- ★ Does he really believe the mill-owners were repeatedly 'ruined' or do you think he is mocking their claims?
- ★ Does he really think it was wrong to send children to school, to make machinery less dangerous and to reduce the amount of smoke? Be prepared to explain your answer.

6 Dickens uses various techniques to make his narrative entertaining and to give his views force. Identify where he uses:
- ★ exaggeration   ★ understatement   ★ repetition.

7 What adjectives might be used to describe Dickens' tone? Decide which of the following might be appropriate or list your own.
- ★ Humorous   ★ Indignant   ★ Critical
- ★ Angry   ★ Relaxed   ★ Uncaring
- ★ Sympathetic   ★ Ironic   ★ Sarcastic

Checklist

checklist

How many points can you add to this list of ways to creat satire?

Ways to create satire

- ✪ Use of exaggeration/understatement
- ✪ Expression of criticism, anger or indignation for someone or something
- ✪ Draw attention to human weakness
- ✪ Build several layers of implied meaning
- ✪ Other ...

Writing

1 Write a short satire (no more than two paragraphs) to criticize a group of people or an organization.

You may give a brief context for your writing, and you should:
★ use an indignant tone to criticize your chosen target
★ include ironic remarks in your writing.

Some suggested targets for your criticism are:
★ people who are cruel to animals, e.g. bad pet owners, fox hunters, research scientists who use them in experiments, etc.
★ people who don't respect the countryside, e.g. who leave litter, build fires, destroy wild life, ignore footpaths, leaves gates open, etc.
★ people who vandalize public property in city centres
★ a topic of your own choice.

2 Discuss your first draft with a partner.
★ Can you explain how the irony in each other's text works?
★ What are the most effective parts of the writing?
★ Suggest ways in which the writing might be sharpened.

3 Redraft your work, then check the spelling and punctuation.

Unit plenary

Discuss:
★ what you have learnt about how tone can be used for effect
★ how you will use this in future writing and speaking tasks.

Additional writing tasks

Short writing task. Write a short satire to criticize an aspect of modern life. Focus on one of the following:
★ our dependence on the car and the traffic problems this produces
★ society's obsession with celebrities, fashion and glamour
★ a topic of your choice.

Longer writing task. Write the opening of a story in which you use a young and innocent first person narrator to amuse the reader and to comment on some aspects of modern life.

Real Writer: Tim Stimpson

Hello! I'm Tim and I write for the world's longest running radio serial, 'The Archers'.

'The Archers' was first broadcast in 1951 as a way of informing farmers about modern agriculture methods to produce more food after World War II. Today the programme has almost five million listeners and they are clearly not all farmers! In order to keep its appeal fresh, the show has had to adapt to suit the changing times and audiences, for example by working contemporary issues, such as the recent Foot-and-Mouth epidemic, into the storyline.

Key to any soap like 'The Archers' are the characters – some of ours have been in the show since it began! Another way in which the programme adapts itself is by showing how these characters react to the changing world and comparing them with the younger generations, so it's vital that these characters remain true to themselves. It's no good me forcing words into their mouths; I have to disappear behind the character so that the listeners believe they are listening to a real person. This sometimes means giving a character a really convincing argument for something you don't actually agree with (extremely hard) or writing dialogue for a nasty character where you say the kind of wicked things you'd never actually dare say yourself (not so hard)!

A good story sets a character some kind of challenge and is most appealing if the audience is unsure whether the character will succeed. It can be great to watch an unlikely character reveal a hidden strength, but sometimes the story works even better if the character fails, as failure is a challenge in itself and seeing how a character deals with it can be just as exciting. Of course, characters in 'The Archers' aren't idealized like those in heroic tales. They are people the audience can relate to, rather than the Gods and monsters of myth and legend.

With all these characters in my head I never find writing a lonely business, and one of the best things about writing for a show like 'The Archers' is that there are ten other writers, as well as the production team and actors, all of whom are working together to create the same imaginary world. Telling stories with friends – what could be better than that?

Objectives

In this unit you will learn how to:

⊛ develop an imaginative or unusual treatment of familiar material or established conventions

⊛ analyse the overall structure of a text to identify how key ideas are developed

⊛ recognize the conventions of some common literary forms

⊛ recognize how texts refer to and reflect the culture in which they were produced.

Introduction

All cultures and societies have their heroes and heroines. Nowadays, we read about our heroes and heroines in books, comics and magazines; we watch programmes about them on TV or films about them at the cinema; we even play games based on these characters.

In the past, stories about heroes and heroines were passed down the generations mainly through the oral tradition (story telling) because few people could read. Story tellers adapted their stories to suit the interests and needs of their audience – this was important if they had to earn their living by pleasing their listeners. Even today, story tellers adapt traditional tales of heroes and heroines to suit new audiences.

This unit looks at how tales of heroes have survived through history, in different cultures, changing to suit different audiences. (The term 'hero' will be used to mean both male and female characters.) You'll look at what these stories have in common, in structure and content, then you'll have a go at writing your own heroic tales, mixing traditional ingredients of the tales with your own interpretation and drawing on your own culture.

What makes a hero?

Activities

discuss

1 In pairs, discuss what makes someone a hero in real life. Jot down two or three names, then explain why you consider them heroic, starting each sentence: 'We think X is a hero/heroine because ...'

2 In the past, the majority of heroes were male, but today many are female. Why do you think this is? Can you think of other differences between modern heroic figures and ancient or historical heroes?

3 Share your ideas with your class, then choose your four top heroes and decide on why you are selecting them.

4 As a group, or pair, write down a possible definition of a 'hero'.

There has to be a public dimension to heroism, but there are plenty of people who are well known and not heroic. To qualify as a hero, a certain amount of valour and fortitude have to be displayed, but by the same token people have to hear about it.

Philip Pullman

A hero is someone who pushes human endeavour further than it has gone previously. Some people do great things out of narrowness or self-interest, but there has to be generosity involved. David Beckham is certainly heroic. He never gives up and carries his team along.

A S Byatt

5 Read and discuss the definitions above. You might also want to look up the definition of 'hero' in a dictionary. What is it's origin?

6 Revise your original definition of a 'hero' to include any new ideas.

7 Look at the following list of characters (some are fictional, some are based on real people). They are from different times and cultures. (You may need to do some research to find out about the ones you are not familiar with.) With a partner, choose six characters and decide:
★ whether these characters fit your definition of a 'hero'
★ what special qualities these characters share
★ how each hero relates to a particular time and culture.
You may think some characters appeal more to children than adults, but whoever they appeal to, most heroes share some qualities.

Lara Croft (from *Tomb Raider*)
Lyra (from *His Dark Materials* trilogy by Philip Pullman)
Harry Potter (from the series by J.K. Rowling)
Hercules (from Greek legend and a recent film)
Gilgamesh (from the Babylonian epic)
Beowulf (from Anglo-Saxon legend)
Ulysses or Odysseus (from Roman and Greek mythology)

continued ...

Indiana Jones (as featured in several films)
King Arthur and his knights (from Arthurian legend)
Frodo Baggins (from *The Lord of the Rings*)
Momotaro (from the Japanese fable)
Kukai (the legendary Japanese Buddhist priest)
Moshoeshoe of Basuto (the African hero)
Robin Hood (from English legend)
Mulan (the Chinese woman warrior)
Nasredin Hodja (the Turkish folk hero)
Buffy the Vampire Slayer (from the television series)
Shrek (from the film)

8 Add more names to your list of heroes. Ask your family, friends and other people in your community about heroes from their culture and other different cultures around the world.

Checklist

Draw up a list of characteristics that your heroes share. How many can you add to the list below?

Characteristics of heroes

- ⭐ Special talent or skill
- ⭐ Courage to meet challenges
- ⭐ Self-sacrificing for others
- ⭐ On the side of justice or good against injustice and evil
- ⭐ Able to push human endeavour to its limits/perseveres in the face of difficulties
- ⭐ Fulfils a destiny or fate
- ⭐ Other characteristics ...

Writing

Now that you have looked at the characteristics that many heroes share, sketch out some ideas for a hero of your own (either invent a hero or choose one that you already know about). Make notes following these steps:

1 Think about the age, gender and cultural background of your hero. (He or she could be from your own culture or any other around the world.)

2 Consider whether they have any special skill or talent.

3 Think about a setting in which he or she can show their heroic qualities (i.e. face them with hardship, conflict or a testing challenge).

4 Decide on the sequence of events that lead up to him or her meeting and overcoming the challenge.

5 Think about how you would portray their relationship with others.

discuss

6 Swap your notes with a partner. Discuss:
   ★ the strengths of each other's work
   ★ areas for development
   ★ whether suitable heroic qualities are displayed by the character (refer back to your checklists).

Keep the notes you have made, as you may wish to use them later on in this unit. You might wish to tell your story to a partner or small group, but make sure you have consolidated your ideas before you begin!

You will now look at how one heroic tale is retold through time.

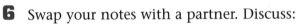
Retelling the traditional hero tale

discuss

Activities

1 What do you know about the story of Perseus? It might not be very much, but share any knowledge you have with the rest of the class or group. Jot down your ideas and use them as a starting point.

2 Now do some further research, using the school library or the Internet:
   ★ When was the story first written down and by whom?
   ★ How would it have survived before it was written down?
   ★ In what language was the story first recorded?
   ★ Is Perseus a fictional or an historical character?
   ★ What are the main events in the story of Perseus?
   ★ Have those events remained the same over time?
   ★ What heroic qualities does Perseus possess?
   ★ How has the story survived to the modern day?

Here is an outline of events in the story of Perseus.

1 King Acrisius of Argos imprisons his daughter, Danae, to prevent her from having children because an oracle has told him that his grandson will grow up to kill him.

2 The god Zeus visits Danae in her prison, disguised as a shower of gold, and the child, Perseus is born.

3 Still worried by the prophecy, Acrisius puts mother and baby into a chest and throws them into the sea.

4 The chest is discovered on the shores of the island of Seriphos whose king, Polydectes, gives them a home.

5 Polydectes wishes to marry Danae, but sees the growing Perseus as a threat to his plans.

6 Polydectes sets Perseus the apparently impossible task of killing the snake-headed female monster, Medusa, whose eyes turn all to stone.

7 With divine help Perseus is armed with winged sandals, a helmet of invisibility, a magic reflective shield and a sharp sickle.

8 Perseus finds and beheads the Gorgon, Medusa, only viewing her in the reflection on his shield.

9 The horse Pegasus and the giant Chrysaor spring from the beheaded Medusa.

10 Returning home, with the Gorgon's head, Perseus rescues a woman called Andromeda from a huge sea monster.

11 Perseus returns to Seriphos to save his mother from being forced into marriage with the evil Polydectes and he uses the Medusa's head to turn his enemies to stone.

12 Later, Perseus takes part in some public games. He throws a discus that accidentally kills an onlooker – his grandfather.

read

You are now going to look at some retellings of one part of this story (part 8 above). As you read, think about why such a story has survived and is still popular today, in retellings, films and even computer games. Also think about how the story has developed and changed through time.

A The first version is a translation from the work of the earliest known writer of the tale, Hesiod, a Greek living in the 8th century B.C. Notice how little of the detail that we now use in telling the tale is included.

The Gorgons ... dwell beyond glorious Ocean in the frontier land towards Night where are the clear-voiced Hesperides, Sthenno, and Euryale, and Medusa who suffered a woeful fate: she was mortal, but the two were undying and grew not old. With her lay the Dark-haired One in a soft meadow amid spring flowers. And when Perseus cut off her head, there sprang forth great Chrysaor and the horse Pegasus who is so called because he was born near the springs of Ocean; and that other, because he held a golden blade in his hands.

B This version was written by Ovid, 800 years later than Hesiod.

Then, by remote and pathless ways, through rocky country thickly overgrown with rough woods, he reached the Gorgon's home. Everywhere, all through the fields and along the roadways he saw statues of men and beast, whom the sight of the Gorgon had changed from their true selves into stone. But he himself looked at the dread Medusa's form as it was reflected in the bronze of the shield which he carried on his left arm. While she and her snakes were wrapped in deep slumber, he severed the head from her shoulders.

C Charles Kingsley extends the tale in his 1856 version.

But Perseus went on boldly, past many an ugly sight, far away into the heart of the Unshapen Land, beyond the streams of Ocean, to the isles where no ship cruises, where it is neither night nor day, where nothing is in its right place, and nothing has a name; till he heard the rustle of the Gorgons' wings and saw the glitter of their brazen talons; and then he knew that it was time to halt, lest Medusa should freeze him into stone.

He thought awhile with himself, and remembered Athene's words. He rose aloft into the air, and held the mirror of the shield above his head, and looked up into it that he might see all that was below him.

And he saw the three Gorgons sleeping as huge as elephants. He knew that they could not see him, because the hat of darkness hid him; and yet he trembled as he sank down near them, so terrible were those brazen claws.

Two of the Gorgons were as foul as swine, and lay sleeping heavily, as swine sleep, with their mighty wings outspread; but Medusa tossed to and fro restlessly, and as she tossed, Perseus pitied her, she looked so fair and sad. Her plumage was like the rainbow, and her face was like the face of a nymph, only her eyebrows were knit, and her lips clenched, with everlasting care and pain; and her long neck gleamed so white in the mirror that Perseus had not the heart to strike, and said, 'Ah, that it had been either of her sisters!'

But as he looked, from among her tresses the vipers' heads awoke, and peeped up with their bright dry eyes, and showed their fangs, and hissed; and Medusa, as she tossed, threw back her wings and showed her brazen claws; and Perseus saw that, for all her beauty, she was as foul and venomous as the rest.

Then he came down and stepped to her boldly, and looked steadfastly on his mirror, and struck with Herpe stoutly once; and he did not need to strike again.

D This final version is by a modern writer, Geraldine McCaughrean.

Even in Hermes' winged sandals, it was a long time before Perseus spotted the Gorgon Medusa's island. It lay below him like a single grey eye in the face of the sea. He did not search about for the monster though; he now knew that one sight of her would turn him to stone. Instead, he found her by the sound of her hair. For he knew that instead of curls or plaits, Medusa's head was crowned with writhing, hissing snakes all spitting poison.

Round about her, a hundred figures still as statues, turned to stone in the very moment that they had first glimpsed Medusa.

'How am I to kill this monster without looking at her?' thought Perseus.

Then the sun flashed on Athene's bright shield and gave him an idea. Holding the shield up in front of his face, he flew backwards. For the first time, he was able to look at the monster, reflected in the shiny metal.

Medusa herself was asleep, though the snakes on her head never slept. They sensed that someone was nearby. They jabbed at the air with forked tongues. But invisible Perseus kicked them aside and swung his sword in a great arc. Medusa's hideous head fell to the ground with a thud.

Activities

1 Do the last three authors give this event a mood of tension and suspense? If so, how and to what extent do they achieve this? Support your answer with evidence from the texts.

2 In such a short piece of writing it can be challenging for a writer to create setting and character. How far does each writer use language to achieve this?

3 What language techniques make the descriptions vivid? List them.

4 Each version presents the main characters in a different way. Compare the way the main characters are presented. Think about:
  ★ adjectives used to describe the character
  ★ the characters' actions and the verbs used to describe them
  ★ figurative language used
  ★ prepositional phrases used
  ★ the characters' words/thoughts.

5 Does each version make you feel the same about Medusa? Or Perseus? Discuss your opinions, justifying your answers to each other.

6 Does the way the story is told in these different versions tell you anything about who it has been written for and when?

Checklist

Draw up a list of the techniques the writers use to make the story of Perseus vivid and compelling. How many points can you add to the list below?

Techniques for retellings

- ✪ Narrative commentary creates mood through carefully selected detail
- ✪ Third person narrative, but the reader often sees events through Perseus' eyes
- ✪ Clear references guide the reader's understanding of character and event in the longer versions, e.g. 'Gorgon Medusa', 'the monster', 'the sound of her hair'
- ✪ Vivid noun phrases, similes and metaphors are used to appeal to the senses
- ✪ Carefully chosen verbs make the action vivid, e.g. 'jabbed'
- ✪ Prepositional phrases add detail, e.g. 'swung his sword *in a great arc*'
- ✪ Repetition and patterns in the language to create mood and pace
- ✪ Other techniques ...

Writing

Think about how a modern retelling of the same story might be updated without losing the basic heroic elements.

Perseus might have to use modern technology to destroy his enemies.

Perseus might travel through outer space to find a thirtieth-century Medusa.

Choose any part of the story of Perseus, and rewrite it for a modern audience (e.g. someone of your own age, a younger/older audience, a film version). Keep your audience in mind as you write, making sure it will appeal. Set your retelling in the culture of your choice.

discuss

Read it aloud to a partner. Together, discuss which features would most appeal to your audience and why.

The structure of the hero quest

think

Activities

1 There are countless stories of heroes across the world, but most of them share a similar plot structure. Return to the list of heroes on pages 44 and 45. What do their stories have in common? With a partner jot down any parallels you can spot between events in the stories.

2 Select one or two heroic tales and compare their structure with the tale of Perseus. Copy and complete the grid on page 52, which uses Harry Potter, and Kestrel from *The Wind Singer* by William Nicholson for comparison. You may wish to choose other stories and heroes.

3 Use the first column of the grid as a checklist of key events of heroic tales. Refer to this list when you are planning your own tale.

4 Try expressing these key events/stages in the form of a time line, using symbols to remind you of each stage of the tale.

Writing your own heroic tale

write

1 Choose or invent a hero for your story. Your hero:
★ can be of any age, gender or culture (think carefully about how you can make the culture come alive)
★ must possess heroic qualities
★ can come from a real or an imaginary place in the past, the present or the future, in this world or another

Think carefully about your chosen audience and what sort of hero will appeal to them.

The classic hero tale	Perseus	Harry Potter	Kestrel
The hero is on a quest to seek out some special object.	Medusa's head	The philosopher's stone	The wind singer
The hero journeys to some strange, terrifying or wonderful land (possibly with several adventures or episodes before the major one).	The island of the Gorgons		
The hero faces a powerful antagonist or some kind of threat.		Voldemort (in disguise as Quirrell)	The Morah, and a society ruled by examinations
The adversary succeeds in imprisoning, enchanting or even killing the hero, but often through a trick, which the hero outwits.	Perseus uses the shield as a mirror to 'look' at Medusa		
The hero overcomes the enemy and despatches or defeats him/her in some gruesome way.	Medusa's head is severed		
The hero gains some reward or recognition, or brings about a change.	Perseus returns to Seriphos	House points, popularity and a feast	

You could research the life of a famous historical figure then turn it into a heroic tale, e.g.

★ In *The Breadwinner*, Deborah Ellis tells the tale of Malali, a small girl whose brave actions won a war in Afghanistan nearly two hundred years ago.

★ Sultana Razia of Delhi led armies in thirteenth century India.

★ The life of the Chinese explorer, Cheng Ho, was very heroic.

2 Using a grid or a time line, plan out the main events in your story. You may alter the basic structure slightly to suit your story and provide a modern twist to appeal to your audience, e.g.

★ You can tell the tale in any order – some Greek writers were fond of flashbacks.

★ The Greeks often ended their tales in tragedy. Your heroic tale does not have to have a happy ending.

★ In the film *Shrek*, the hero sets out upon a quest with his donkey helper. The story reverses the conventions of the characters – a monstrous hero, a karate expert for a princess and a harmless dragon.

Share your plans with a partner or group and discuss how the traditional structure helps you to map out the story. Think about:
★ how it would help you remember the story if it was not written down
★ how you could adapt the story to suit another audience very quickly
★ how you could make someone else's story your own by changing around names and details.

3 Write a first draft. Refer back to the checklist on page 50.

4 Try out your first draft on a partner. Look for two positive features in each other's work, and find one feature that could be improved.

5 Before completing a final draft, check your spelling and punctuation.

Unit plenary

What makes a hero in literature? In what ways has your exploration of heroic figures in literature altered your ideas of the hero in real life? Why do we keep creating heroes and legends?

Additional writing tasks

1 **Short writing task**. Create a contemporary hero from any culture who will challenge a modern monster. Remember, the 'monster' can be any of the difficult challenges that you meet as you journey through life. Tell the opening of this story.

2 **Longer writing task**. Using some of the writing that you have already done in this unit, extend your work into a full heroic tale.

Real Writer: John Hegley

He went off to sea from Australia to the Bahamas
an excellent seaman, who <u>did</u> like to be in his bunk,
he went off to sea in a pair of his father's pyjamas,
he also went off in a boat or he may well have sunk.

Hi, I'm John Hegley and I'm a poet and so is my dog. Most of my poetry uses rhyme. Sometimes it's pairs of lines rhyming together and sometimes, like the lines above, it rhymes every other line. Occasionally I'll try a Haiku – a tiny pebble of a poem, which usually has a line with five syllables, then a line with seven, and finally one more with five. This one's a bit short:

Reading this poem
you, whom I may never know;
HELLO.

I once wanted to write something about what a poem is. I was finding this difficult, so decided to write about what a poem is *not*. The form I used was alphabetical. It began 'A poem is not an Ant but it can be quite short'. After Ant came Banana, Coat, Dog, Endless pair of trousers and so on. The last two lines were:

A poem is not a Year old bag of vegetables
but it can smell quite strongly;
A poem is not a Zylophone
and it can spell words wrongly.

I write quite a lot of limericks too. A limerick is thought of as quite a silly form, so sometimes I try to use it to say something sensible or sad. And because it is such a well-worn way of writing, I try to go off in unusual directions:

There once was a creature from space
who entered a three-legged race.
He was not very fast
in fact he came last
because he was a bag of oven-ready chips.

I often try to vary things. Attempt to surprise. But not always. Or it wouldn't be surprising. Using these forms gets me to come up with words and ideas I wouldn't have considered otherwise. The acrostic does this even more. An example of an acrostic with the word LOVE is:

Lot Of Valentines Envelopes.

I also did one which I called 'The Donkey Dentist':

Please Open Ee-aw Mouth.

Form can be fun!

Objectives

In this unit you will learn how to:

⭐ experiment with figurative language in conveying a sense of character and setting

⭐ experiment with presenting similar material in different forms and styles of poetry

⭐ investigate the different ways familiar themes are explored and presented by different writers.

Introduction

Poems come in all shapes and sizes and can be about anything and everything. The form a poem takes depends on how the poet chooses to present his ideas – it's a matter of personal taste. So while several poets might decide to write about snow, for example, the chances that two of them will come up with exactly the same poem are extremely slim.

In this unit, you'll be looking at how different poets write about the sea and the form they choose to present their ideas. You'll also examine how poets use figurative language to create a vivid impression of the setting for the reader, as well as how they offer the reader additional images through the techniques of simile and metaphor. Techniques such as these can help a poem to come to life for a reader and in this unit you'll be experimenting with your own use of figurative language too.

starter

Starter activity

With a partner read and discuss the following extracts then decide:
★ how the writer has presented the image of the sea
★ what techniques the poet has employed to create the image.
Record your observations in a table like the one opposite.

A Daybreak is breaking
On the green chrome water,

'A Sea Chantey' by Derek Walcott

C you are the waves
which cover my feet like cold eiderdowns

'What You Are' by Roger McGough

B It has hard whips
That it cracks, and knuckles
To pummel you. It scrubs
And scours; it chews rocks
To sand;

'The Sea' by R S Thomas

E Thick skinned in wetsuits, sitting on surf boards,
we are learning to read again,
tracing, in the distance, the phrases of the waves.

'Sea Reading' by Owen Sheers

D a sea breathes in and out
upon a shore.

'Until I Saw the Sea'
by Lilian Moore

F Hurricane come
And hurricane go
but sea ... sea timeless
sea timeless
sea timeless
sea timeless

'Sea Timeless Song' by
Grace Nichols

G The slow, sad murmur of far distant seas
Whipped by an icy breeze
Upon a shore
Wind-swept and desolate.

'The Shell' by James Stephens

simile – a form of imagery that compares something like or as something else

metaphor – a form of imagery where something is said to be something else

Extract	Image of the sea	Techniques employed by the poet (figurative language)
A	Still, as day breaks	Metaphor – describing the water as green chrome (a shiny silver metal) is a powerful image. The reader can visualize the sea as still and the early light reflecting off the surface of the metal.
B		Metaphor – describing the sea when there is a storm; use of onomatopoeia to create the sound effects of the sea.
C		

onomatopoeia – the effect created by words which reflect the sounds associated with their meaning, e.g. crack, hiss

alliteration – the effect created when words begin with the same initial sound, e.g. several silent, slithering snakes

repetition – repeating a word or phrase for particular effect

Style and technique

read

Read the poem 'Until I Saw the Sea' by Lilian Moore carefully twice.

Until I Saw the Sea

Until I saw the sea
I did not know
that wind
could wrinkle water so.

I never knew
that sun
could splinter a whole sea of blue.

Nor
did I know before
a sea breathes in and out
upon a shore.

Activities

think

1 What image is the poet creating of the sea? Try to sum this up in just a few words.

2 How does the poet create the image? Think about:
   ★ the structure of the poem – e.g. the number of verses, the rhyme scheme, etc.
   ★ the techniques used to build the image – e.g. the use of alliteration, metaphor, simile, personification, etc.
   ★ the way the techniques appeal to the senses – what you can hear, see, feel, etc.

3 How does the poet create these effects? (Think about the use of verbs.)

read   Read through 'The Sea' by James Reeves carefully twice.

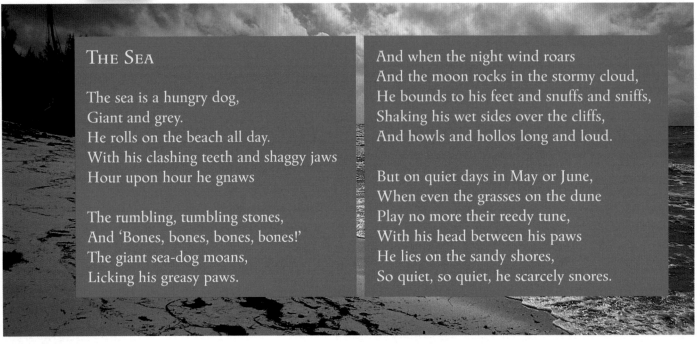

THE SEA

The sea is a hungry dog,
Giant and grey.
He rolls on the beach all day.
With his clashing teeth and shaggy jaws
Hour upon hour he gnaws

The rumbling, tumbling stones,
And 'Bones, bones, bones, bones!'
The giant sea-dog moans,
Licking his greasy paws.

And when the night wind roars
And the moon rocks in the stormy cloud,
He bounds to his feet and snuffs and sniffs,
Shaking his wet sides over the cliffs,
And howls and hollos long and loud.

But on quiet days in May or June,
When even the grasses on the dune
Play no more their reedy tune,
With his head between his paws
He lies on the sandy shores,
So quiet, so quiet, he scarcely snores.

Activities

think

1 How does the poet describe the sea?

2 How does the poet adapt this image to show how the sea changes?

3 How does the poet create the image? Think about:
   ★ the structure of the poem – e.g. the number of verses, the rhyme scheme, etc.
   ★ the techniques used to build the image – e.g. the use of alliteration, metaphor, simile, personification, etc.
   ★ the way the techniques appeal to the senses – what you can hear, see, feel, etc.

4 Draw a quick sketch to show the scene the poet has created. Identify key points in your sketch with quotes from the poem.

discuss

5 In pairs, brainstorm other images you could use to represent the sea. How could they be adapted to show the changes to the sea?

6 You have now explored two very different poems based on a similar theme. Think about the similarities and differences between the poems. Compare the images created, the structure and the techniques used.

checklist

Checklist

Start a checklist of techniques you might use to write effective poetry.

Poetic techniques

- ⭐ Variety of structure and line length
- ⭐ Similes and metaphors help the reader to imagine the scene
- ⭐ Personification adds impact to the images created by the poet
- ⭐ Alliteration adds to the imagery and aural quality of the poem
- ⭐ Use of an extended image
- ⭐ Other techniques ...

write

Now use some of these techniques to create a poetic image of the sea.

1 Decide what sort of state the sea is going to be in when you describe it.

2 Decide on two or three images you want to create. What do you want your reader to be able to see, hear, feel?

3 Brainstorm techniques you can use to create these images. Remember:
- ★ you can create a sense of sound through onomatopoeia; a sense of sight through similes and metaphors; and feelings through a combination of figurative techniques
- ★ to choose appropriate verbs, adverbs and nouns to create a variety of effects
- ★ NOT to use figurative language just for the sake of it – make sure it does some work!

4 Experiment with the images – rework them, trying out different techniques, to produce the image that you want.

discuss

5 Share your ideas with a partner. Ask him or her to comment on the images you have produced and to make any suggestions on how you could develop them further. Do the same for your partner.

6 Produce a fresh draft of your images, taking into account the feedback your partner has offered in step 5. Keep your ideas carefully as you may want to refer to them as you work through this unit.

Ballads

read

A ballad is a poem that tells a story. Ballads are often written in verses of four lines, which have a regular rhyme scheme.

rhyme scheme – the patterns of rhymes in a verse when the endings of words share the same sounds

The following extract comes from *The Rime of the Ancient Mariner* by Samuel Taylor Coleridge, written in 1798. The poem opens with a wedding. One of the guests is stopped by an old sailor (the ancient mariner of the title), who tells the tale of how he set sail one fine day, heading south. All was going well until a storm broke. Read through the extract carefully twice.

And now the Storm-blast came, and he
Was tyrannous and strong:
He struck with his o'ertaking wings,
And chased us south along.

With sloping masts and dipping prow,
As who pursued with yell and blow
Still treads the shadow of his foe
And forward bends his head,
The ship drove fast, loud roared the blast,
And southward aye we fled.

And now there came both mist and snow,
And it grew wondrous cold:
And ice, mast-high, came floating by,
As green as emerald.

And through the drifts the snowy clifts
Did send a dismal sheen:
Nor shapes of men nor beasts we ken —
The ice was all between.

The ice was here, the ice was there,
The ice was all around:
It cracked and growled, and roared and howled,
Like noises in a swound!

At length did cross an Albatross:
Thorough the fog it came;
As if it had been a Christian soul,
We hailed it in God's name.

It ate the food it ne'er had eat,
And round and round it flew.
The ice did split with a thunder-fit;
The helmsman steered us through!

And a good south wind sprung up behind;
The Albatross did follow,
And every day, for food or play,
Came to the mariners' hollo!

In mist or cloud, on mast or shroud,
It perched for vespers nine;
Whiles all the night, through fog-smoke white,
Glimmered the white Moon-shine.

'God save thee, ancient Mariner!
From the fiends, that plague thee thus! –
Why look'st thou so?' – With my cross-bow
I shot the ALBATROSS.

Glossary

aye – always
sheen – soft shine
swound – swoon or faint
shroud – a length of cloth in which a dead person is **wrapped** for burial
vesper – evening prayer

think

Activities

1 How is the storm described?

2 What effect does the storm have on the ship?

3 What happens after the storm? Think about:
   ★ how this is described
   ★ the techniques Coleridge uses to build up a picture of the ice
   ★ the use of simile, metaphor, alliteration, onomatopoeia, etc. – how are these figurative techniques used to appeal to the senses?

4 Explore the rhyme scheme by coding the lines that rhyme with the same letter. The first verse has the rhyme scheme *abcb* – do all the verses follow this pattern?

5 Draw a rough sketch that shows the situation the ship is in. Label the relevant part of the sketch with key quotes from the ballad.

6 What effect does the arrival of the albatross have?

7 *The Rime of the Ancient Mariner* is an example of a ballad. Does it follow the typical rhyme scheme of a ballad? If not, does it follow a rhyme scheme at all and, if so, what is it?

8 The above extract is taken from early on in Coleridge's ballad. Think about how the narrative might continue. Jot down a few ideas.

9 *The Rime of the Ancient Mariner* was written in 1798. What are some of the challenges you encountered when reading this poem? How did you go about working out unfamiliar vocabulary?

checklist

Checklist

Begin a checklist of features of the ballad form. How many features can you add to the list started for you below?

Ballads:

⊕ Tell a story
⊕ Written in verses which may be four lines long
⊕ The verses may follow the rhyme scheme *aabb*
⊕ The poet may use a range of techniques to create strong images for the reader – e.g. alliteration, simile, metaphor, etc.
⊕ Other features ...

write

Writing

Following the structure of *The Rime of the Ancient Mariner*, and using some of Coleridge's techniques, write two or three verses to describe the ship at sea.

> **1** Choose one of the following options:
> ★ No longer at a standstill, the ship is making steady progress.
> ★ The ship is still unable to progress because of the lack of wind.

> **2** Think about:
> ★ how you are going to describe the ship
> ★ the sort of effects you want to create
> ★ the techniques you are going to use to achieve those effects.
> You may find it helpful to start by drawing a rough sketch of the image you want to portray in words. Then, experiment by adding key words to the sketch before you attempt to draft your verses.

> **3** Draft your verses. Think carefully about the effects you want to achieve.

discuss

> **4** Share your ideas with a partner. Ask him or her to comment on the powerful images you have used and to make suggestions about aspects that could be developed further.

> **5** Revise your verses, taking your partner's comments into account. Be prepared to share your work with the rest of the class.

Sonnets

read

A sonnet is a poem with fourteen lines, each of which usually has ten syllables and a basic pattern of stressed and unstressed syllables.

Read through the sonnet by John Keats on page 63 carefully twice.

Glossary

gluts – fills up
Hecate – goddess of the moon
vex'd – strained
start – are startled
quir'd – sang

On the Sea

It keeps eternal whisperings around
   Desolate shores, and with its mighty swell
   Gluts twice ten thousand caverns; till the spell
Of Hecate leaves them their old shadowy sound.
Often 'tis in such gentle temper found,
   That scarcely will the very smallest shell
   Be mov'd for days from where it sometime fell,
When last the winds of heaven were unbound.
Oh ye who have your eye-balls vex'd and tir'd
   Feast them upon the wideness of the sea;
   Oh ye whose ears are dinn'd with uproar rude,
   Or fed too much with cloying melody –
   Sit ye near some old cavern's mouth and brood
Until ye start, as if the sea-nymphs quir'd!

think

Activities

1 Look at how the poet describes the sea. Pick out key quotes from the text that create a strong image for the reader

2 What other techniques does the poet use to present the image?

3 Work out the rhyme scheme. (You can do this by giving each new rhyme the next letter of the alphabet – e.g. the first four lines of this sonnet can be represented as *abba*.

checklist

Checklist

Make a checklist of the features of the sonnet form. If you wish, use the list below as a starting point. How many features can you add?

Sonnets:

- ✪ Have 14 lines
- ✪ Each line usually has ten syllables and the basic pattern of stressed and unstressed syllables
- ✪ May end with a rhyming couplet that resolves or reserves an issue
- ✪ The poet may use a range of techniques to develop the image
- ✪ Other features …

write

Write your own sonnet about the sea.

> **1** Brainstorm some ideas to develop your feelings about the sea. You might find it useful to explore the different moods of the sea and your responses to each of them.

> **2** Try out some of your ideas in verse. You may need to vary the line lengths to support your ideas.

> **3** Write a first draft of your sonnet. You may find it helpful to use the following lines as a starting point (you can always rewrite these lines when your own sonnet is more developed):
>
> **Beyond the Sea**
>   The distant call of the waves draws me in
>   The whispering of the pebbles grows louder
>   The regular breathing of the bold sea
>   conceals the ancient secrets in the fathomless deep

discuss

> **4** Swap your work with a partner and give each other feedback.

> **5** Prepare a revised draft of your sonnet, then share it with the rest of the class. Ask for comments and suggestions.

think

Activity: Creating different effects

Explore a theme of your choice – e.g. the sun, the wind, autumn, etc. Experiment with different forms and styles of poetry.

> **1** Decide on the subject you are going to explore.

> **2** Brainstorm all your ideas associated with the subject you have chosen.

> **3** Experiment with a range of forms, styles and techniques to build a picture of the subject you have chosen.

discuss

4 Develop some of these examples into two or three verses, or into a sonnet.

5 Share your work with a partner and ask for feedback.

6 Rework a selection of your ideas to create a final draft of the poem of your choice. Be prepared to share your work with the rest of the class.

Unit plenary

discuss

Revisit and discuss the work you have completed as part of this unit. Check your understanding of the forms and styles of the poems you have explored. Pick out an image you find particularly powerful from the extracts in this unit and work out what makes it so effective for you.

Additional writing tasks

write

1 **Short writing task**. Write a short poem, choosing the form you feel is most appropriate. In your poem, explore the feelings you get either at the start of term or at the start of a holiday. Use a range of techniques to allow the reader to empathize with your feelings.

2 **Longer writing task**. Write a ballad in which you explore a local story or event. You will need to have a clear idea of the story before you begin to work it into the form of a ballad.

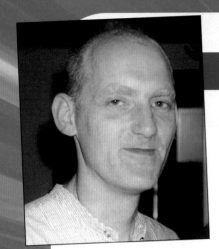

Real Writer: Andy Solway

Hi, I'm Andy Solway. I write books about all sorts of things, from the viruses you can find up your nose to what it was like to live in ancient Rome. Most things I write are for children or young adults.

When you write information books you have to be sure to get your facts straight, so I spend a lot of my time doing research. The Internet is usually a good place to start, but I also use all kinds of libraries. You need to do a lot of research for even a simple information book – you have to try and really understand a subject before you can write about it successfully.

It's also really useful to talk to people who are experts in the subject you are writing about. When I was writing an illustrated book about Rome, the illustrator and I bombarded the two experts who were helping us with questions: Did the Romans have cranes? What did they look like? How much weight could they carry?

You need to remember your audience too. For example, if you want to discuss DNA or the atomic nucleus in a book for eight year olds, you have to do quite a lot of explaining so that they know what you are talking about. On the other hand, if you make things too simple, your readers will think it's babyish.

What I love about my job is the challenge of getting your head around a subject (which can be pretty tricky if you're writing about atomic physics!) and then finding a way to explain it clearly and simply. I also just enjoy finding out new things. Something that sounds as if it is going to be really boring can turn out to be fascinating once you learn a bit more about it. For example, did you know that there are over 100 different kinds of virus up your nose …

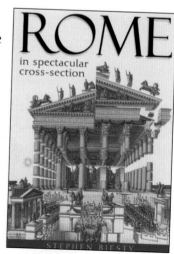

Objectives

In this unit you will learn how to:
- ✪ organize and present information, selecting material and guiding the reader clearly through the text, e.g. an information leaflet
- ✪ explain complex ideas and information clearly.

Introduction

Have you ever tried to find some information, waded through masses of text and ended up more baffled and confused than when you started?

When you write to communicate information, it is vital that you consider the needs of your reader very carefully. Will the reader understand what you have written? Have you explained it clearly enough? Will the reader be able to digest the information and remember it?

In this unit you will be developing your ability to organize and present written information for different audiences and purposes, as well as looking at how to go about explaining complex ideas.

Starter activity

With a partner quickly brainstorm some of the different ways in which published information is presented to you and jot down a few notes. Remember the wide range of information texts available, e.g. school textbooks, leaflets about historical sites, information about a new computer game, newspaper articles about important world events, etc. For each type of information text, think about:

- ★ how the ideas are expressed, and ordered or sequenced
- ★ how difficult words and ideas are explained
- ★ how the ideas are presented in terms of print size and style
- ★ the use of colour, diagram and illustration.

Organize and present

The way information is organized varies from text to text, but a successful information text is always organized in a clear, logical way to the reader.

think

Activity

The text below is from a British Nutrition Foundation poster. The title of the poster title is *Cook-Chill Chain*. In the shortest possible time identify the introduction, then put the captions into the correct order.

10°C - 15°C
ASSEMBLY AND PACKING
The food is assembled and packed in a temperature controlled environment of a maximum of 15°C. The food is kept below 10°C.

0°C - 8°C
SUPERMARKET
The product is kept in refrigerated display cabinets between 0°C - 5°C for optimum quality (maximum 8°C for safety).

5°C - 8°C
RAPID COOLING
The pasta is water chilled to 5°C. The sauce is forced air-chilled to below 10°C in less than 2 hours, then as quickly as possible to 5°C.

SPAGHETTI BOLOGNESE
The manufacture of any cook-chill product is monitored throughout preparation, distribution and sale for quality, hygiene and safety. Food at temperatures between 5°C and 63°C for long periods of time are at risk, as micro-organisms can easily multiply. Monitoring and controlling temperature and time can help prevent this from occurring.

72°C - 100°C
REHEATING
The product should be reheated following pack instructions, to achieve a core temperature of at least 72°C.

0°C - 8°C
DISPATCH & DISTRIBUTION
The products are dispatched in temperature controlled vehicles to stores, which maintain food at 0°C - 8°C.

5°C
COOLING
The product is air-chilled to below 5°C in approximately 30 minutes.

100°C
SAUCE & PASTA PREPARATION AND COOKING
The pasta (egg and semolina) is prepared and pasteurised for 4 minutes. The sauce (meat, vegetables and herbs) is prepared and cooked for 2 hours to develop flavour.

Activities

1 In pairs discuss what helped you to decide on your final order.
   ★ How did you identify the introduction?
   ★ How did the headings help you to sequence the points?
   ★ What else did you notice about the style of writing?
   ★ What sort of vocabulary is used?
   ★ Is the text written in the active or passive voice?
   ★ Which tense of verb is used?

2 This information forms part of an information poster. What other presentational features do you think might be necessary for the reader to be attracted to and guided through its contents? Share your thoughts.

3 Look at the reproduction of the *Cook-Chill Chain* poster on page 70. Is the information more accessible in this format? Why? Think about:
   ★ use of colour and pictures
   ★ use of arrows and numbered boxes.

Writing

Imagine that the information in the *Cook-Chill Chain* poster had to be presented without any visuals, design or colour, but written in straightforward paragraphs. What changes would you have to make in order to be sure that the explanation remained clear? Think about:
★   how to sequence the ideas
★   how to signpost the topic of each paragraph without a sub-heading.
Now try to write this information text. Follow these steps:

1 Jot down five connectives that can be used to sequence paragraphs for a process or explanation.

2 Choose three consecutive stages in the *Cook-Chill Chain*. You may not choose the introduction.

3 Write topic sentences for your chosen stages, using suitable connectives to link one stage to the next.

4 Write a first draft of your chosen paragraphs, following the information provided in the relevant stages of the *Cook-Chill Chain*.

Which format is more efficient: straight text or colourful poster?

COOK-CHILL CHAIN

BRITISH Nutrition FOUNDATION

MAFF
Ministry of Agriculture Fisheries and Food

SPAGHETTI BOLOGNESE

The manufacture of any cook-chill product is monitored throughout preparation, distribution and sale for quality, hygiene and safety. Food at temperatures between 5°C and 63°C for long periods of time are at risk, as micro-organisms can easily multiply. Monitoring and controlling temperature and time can help prevent this from occurring.

1 100°C
SAUCE & PASTA PREPARATION AND COOKING
The pasta (egg and semolina) is prepared and pasteurised for 4 minutes. The sauce (meat, vegetables and herbs) is prepared and cooked for 2 hours to develop flavour.

2 5°C - 8°C
RAPID COOLING
The pasta is water chilled to 5°C. The sauce is forced air-chilled to below 10°C in less than 2 hours, then as quickly as possible to 5°C.

3 10°C - 15°C
ASSEMBLY AND PACKING
The food is assembled and packed in a temperature controlled environment of a maximum of 15°C. The food is kept below 10°C.

4 5°C
COOLING
The product is air-chilled to below 5°C in approximately 30 minutes.

5 0°C - 8°C
DISPATCH & DISTRIBUTION
The products are dispatched in temperature controlled vehicles to stores, which maintain food at 0°C - 8°C.

6 0°C - 8°C
SUPERMARKET
The product is kept in refrigerated display cabinets between 0°C - 5°C for optimum quality (maximum 8°C for safety).

7 72°C - 100°C
REHEATING
The product should be reheated following pack instructions, to achieve a core temperature of at least 72°C.

HOT — TEMPERATURE — COLD

ONE DAY | 12-18 HOURS | UP TO 5 DAYS

Checklist

Begin a checklist of the features of an informative poster that seeks to explain a technological process. You may wish to use the list below as a starting point. How many features can you add?

Features of an informative poster

- ✪ Pictures and colour contribute to the understanding of stages and appeal to the eye
- ✪ A clear, unambiguous title
- ✪ An introductory caption/paragraph indicates the main subject
- ✪ Headings clarify the stages or order the information
- ✪ Points are sequenced logically, e.g. in a flow chart
- ✪ Present tense and passive voice are used
- ✪ Impersonal and formal language is used
- ✪ Other features ...

Skim read the text on page 72, an information leaflet from the RSPCA.

Activities

1 What is the purpose of this leaflet?

2 Who is the intended audience?

3 In what way does the selection of material and the way it is arranged in the leaflet suit that purpose and audience?

4 With a partner, look at the leaflet in more detail. On an A4 sheet of paper, draw a plan or diagram of the leaflet to show how the space has been used, then:
  - ★ label each area of the plan according to whether it is a picture, diagram or text
  - ★ for the text areas write a word or phrase to summarize the topic covered in that particular space
  - ★ where the use of colour or font size and style are noticeable, indicate that in your plan.

5 When you have finished your plan, consider the following questions:
  - ★ What is the proportion of text to image?
  - ★ How does written text relate to image?
  - ★ How has font size and style been used to guide the reader's attention?

Frogs and toads

RSPCA Information

the facts

RSPCA

What's the difference?

Common frogs

- have smooth, moist skin which is not slimy
- have special glands to keep the skin moist and supple – this helps them to 'breathe' through their skin as well as their lungs so that they can stay underwater for a long time
- are mottled shades of green, yellow or brown
- have a distinct brown patch behind the eye
- move in springy leaps.

Common toads

- have a dry warty skin which means they can't 'breathe' through their skin as well as frogs but they can survive on land in drier places
- are usually grey-brown
- crawl rather than hop.

In your garden?

Garden ponds have become increasingly important as mini nature reserves for frogs and toads since, throughout the countryside, large numbers of ponds have either been filled in, allowed to silt up or become polluted.

A thoughtfully constucted pond will attract frogs and toads

Floating plants: for cover

Marshy margins for warmer areas of water which encourage faster spawn development

60cm deep (minimum) for hibernation in mud at pond bottom

Rockery for hibernation

Overhanging plants for cover

Where do they hibernate?

During the autumn, as night-time temperatures drop towards freezing point, frogs and toads look for winter quarters. Female and immature frogs and most toads overwinter on land in sheltered places such as under old logs or in stone walls. Most male frogs return to the water and lie dormant at the bottom of the pond. If the pond freezes over for a long time, there may be problems for the frogs – they will suffocate when all the oxygen in the water has been used. This risk can be reduced by regularly melting the ice on part of the pond by placing a pan of hot water on it. This method cuts out the possibility of shock waves harming the pond inhabitants.

DANGERS to frogs and toads

Garden hazards!

Frogs and toads are frequently the victims of careless strimming and mowing, especially in grass that is not kept closely mown. Nylon garden netting, used to protect fruit and vegetables can trap and slowly kill amphibians as well as other wildlife.

For ¾ mile

Stop! Toads crossing

In the spring, toads often migrate in large groups and over distances of a kilometre or more in order to return to their pond to breed. When they cross roads, many get squashed by cars. You can help by carrying them across.

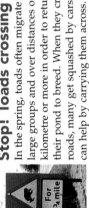

RSPCA

Wilberforce Way
Southwater, Horsham
West Sussex RH13 9RS
Tel: 0870 010 1181
www.rspca.org.uk
Registered Charity No. 219099
We receive no government funding

★ What other techniques have been used to make the text digestible for the reader? Think about the features of the written text, such as paragraphing, sentence type and length, vocabulary, etc.
★ Is this text impersonal and formal? Does it use the active or the passive voice?
★ Does the text do more than inform the reader?
★ If you had to turn this text into paragraphs of writing only, what would you use as your introduction and topic sentences?

Checklist

Begin to put together a checklist of the features of an informative leaflet like the one started for you below. See how many features you can add.

> ### Features of an informative leaflet
>
> ✪ A clear, large title that says what the text is about, and a charity logo
> ✪ Equal amounts of linked illustration and text in the central folds
> ✪ Headings in colour and different font styles – these can be questions to stimulate curiosity
> ✪ Bullet points for descriptive lists
> ✪ Language is not technical, and can be informal
> ✪ A variety of sentence types
> ✪ Sometimes the information offers advice or persuades the reader
> ✪ Addresses and other details
> ✪ Other features ...

Writing

Design and write an information leaflet on a wild animal of your choice:
★ Research your choice – the RSPCA leaflet above provides a good model of the sorts of information you will need to collect.
★ Use your plan of the *Frogs and Toads* leaflet as a note-making frame.
★ Find illustrations and/or diagrams of your chosen creature.
★ Be prepared to share your finished work with the class.

Explaining complex ideas

discuss

Brainstorm what you know about the people believed to be responsible for the destruction of the World Trade Centre in Manhattan, New York, on September 11, 2001.

The following article appeared in a newspaper designed for secondary school students in October 2001. It aims to explain some of the reasons for the events that occurred on 11 September 2001. Read it through carefully.

So what's it all about?

In an attempt to explain recent world events, The Newspaper *team looks at the key players involved in the crisis and some possible reasons for the attacks on the World Trade Centre.*

Osama bin Laden has been blamed by the west for the horrific attacks in New York, but just who is he? Osama bin Laden is the wealthy son of a rich family from Saudi Arabia and is now believed to be hiding in Afghanistan.

In the 1980s he was a commander in Afghanistan, leading attacks against the old Soviet Union. The Soviets had invaded because Afghanistan, a very poor country, was in a region of the world that they wanted to control.

Bin Laden was fighting what he saw as a holy war, or *jihad*. He still claims to be fighting for Islam. He believes America is still trying to dominate the Muslim world and is reported to think no act of killing is too harsh against those he sees as the enemies of Islam.

After the Soviets gave up and left Afghanistan, bin Laden set up his own terrorist network, al-Qaida. A terrorist is a man or woman who uses terror to get his or her own way. A terrorist's aim is to spread fear and death for political gain.

Osama bin Laden is believed to be behind the 11 September attacks and also is suspected of the earlier bombings of US buildings in Africa, in which many Americans and Africans died. His most fanatical supporters are content to die for a cause, confident they will be rewarded in the after-life.

Who are the Taliban?

The name Taliban means student of religion and refers to the group of men who have been governing Afghanistan. They sprang from religious schools in Pakistan and swept into Afghanistan in 1992 after the Soviets left. At first they were welcomed.

The Taliban insist that Afghans follow the harshest form of Islam, and their laws are very strict. Girls are not allowed to go to school. Women are not allowed to earn money or even allowed to show their faces in public. When they go out they must wear a burka – a dress that covers them from head to toe. If they are seen by the Taliban with any part of their body showing they are punished. Men must grow beards and obey the strictest laws of the Taliban in public, without trial and for little reason. Thousands have fled Afghanistan, some because they were starving, others for fear of the bombing and others for fear of the Taliban.

think

checklist

Activities

1 Who is Osama bin Laden?
   ★ Pick out key words and their definitions as given in the text – how does the writer make these explanations clear?
   ★ Comment on the types of sentences used by the writer – how do these help the reader to understand the text?
   ★ List the four main points made about Osama bin Laden.
   ★ How has the writer organized the text to make it clear?

2 Who are the Taliban?
   ★ Pick out key words and their definitions as given in the text – how does the writer make these explanations clear?
   ★ Comment on the types of sentences used by the writer – how do these help the reader to understand the text?
   ★ What is harsh about the Taliban laws? List five points.
   ★ How has the writer expressed these ideas to help the reader?

3 The whole text
   ★ What did you most like about this piece of writing?
   ★ How has the writer made this text easier for you to understand? Think about features of layout, language, illustration, etc.

Checklist

A list of the features of newspaper information texts has been started for you below. Add as many features as you can.

Features of newspaper information texts

✪ An introductory sentence or two to give the reader a context for the article or some idea of what will follow
✪ Headings to guide the reader through the different ideas
✪ Clear paragraphing – a specific topic for each
✪ Logical order of points – connectives help to develop this logic
✪ Sentences are varied, but never over-complicated
✪ Vocabulary is either explained or easily understood
✪ Text is presented in a readable form with appropriate illustration
✪ Other features ...

Writing

The Newspaper team have asked you to write three or four paragraphs updating their readers about Osama bin Laden and his Taliban. The maximum you can write is four paragraphs, including an introductory paragraph and brief conclusion. You must address a maximum of three clearly signposted topics.

Before you start to write, you will need to do some research to find the latest information about the topic. You might like to use these questions to guide your research:

★ What happened in Afghanistan during and after the war there in 2001/2002?
★ What has happened to the Taliban since 2001?
★ What is life like for girls and women in Afghanistan now?
★ Who rules Afghanistan now?
★ What has happened to Osama bin Laden?

1 Research the topic. Use skimming and scanning skills to search for facts and opinions. Share useful sources of information with the class.

2 Select, synthesize and organize the information. Think about:
★ what title or sub-titles you will use
★ how you will begin your article to set the scene and link to the previous article
★ what connectives you will use a) to link your paragraphs, and b) to link sentences within your paragraphs
★ how you will conclude your article.

3 Write a first draft. Ask a partner to read your work. Check that:
★ it makes sense
★ it explains complex ideas clearly
★ it is interestingly expressed.

4 Check for errors in expression, punctuation or spelling. Decide on the best way of presenting your article.

5 Complete a final draft. Be prepared to share your work with the class.

Unit plenary

discuss

Discuss:
★ what you have learnt about organizing and presenting information
★ the different ways in which you have worked with information texts
★ how you have guided the reader in your own information texts
★ what you have learnt that will help you to read other information texts with more understanding.

Additional writing tasks

write

1 **Short writing task.** When you were in Year 7, there were many routines in your school that you had to learn in order to be successful or avoid trouble – for example, how the merit or reward system works, how to use the school library, etc.

Write a short and helpful explanation of a process that is particular to your school and that might help a new Year 7 student. Keep it really simple and use diagrams as well as words if you wish.

2 **Longer writing task.** Television programmes in which contestants compete for attractive prizes and rewards are very popular – e.g. 'Big Brother', 'Who Wants to be a Millionaire', etc.

Choose one of these programmes and write a clear explanation of how it is organized from the beginning through to the final stage of congratulating the winner. Your target audience is an adult who does not watch television regularly. Remember:
★ plan the stages of the explanation
★ keep to the important points
★ explain any specialist language.

Real Writer: Tom Parkinson

Hi! My name's Tom Parkinson and I'm a freelance travel writer. For the last couple of years I've been working for Lonely Planet, the biggest independent guidebook publisher in the world. My job is to update travel guidebooks – I visit a country, collect all the information I can, and then rewrite the old book to make it as accurate as possible.

Obviously the research is the fun part, but it's a lot of legwork. I spend most of my time abroad visiting hotels, restaurants, museums, bars and anything else I think is interesting. Everywhere I go, I take notes and these – and there's always a lot of them! – are really important, as they contain all the facts and figures I'll need for the write-up.

Writing this kind of description text is a balancing act. All the information has to be included in the right place and presented in a certain way to make it easy to find, but at the same time the text has to be interesting for the reader, not just a list of addresses. Using unusual adjectives is a great way of making something stand out, and all travel writers love finding funny or bizarre stories they can use to liven things up a bit.

It's important to get the balance right as there's a lot of competition and travellers are very fussy – our readers come from all over the world, and we have to try and please them all!

I enjoy my job because it gives me incredible opportunities to travel: I visited Africa three times last year, and am working in Europe at the moment. As a writer, though, it's most satisfying to see your name at the front of the finished book and know that travellers are following your advice, and your footsteps, round the world!

www.lonelyplanet.com

Objectives

In this unit you will learn how to:
- ❂ describe an event, process or situation, using language with an appropriate degree of formality
- ❂ review your developing skills as an active, critical reader who searches for meaning using a range of reading strategies.

Introduction

Imagine listening to a football commentary on the radio where the commentators don't describe what's happening on the pitch. How would you know who's got the ball, what they're doing with it, who's about to score? Without a description, how do you picture the scene? Without a description, would you keep listening?

Description is what draws a listener or reader into the scene. In this unit you'll be exploring how writers create descriptions of events, processes and situations. An **event** – an action or chain of actions – might be a football match, for example, while a **situation** – usually more reflective – might be the atmosphere after the match has finished. By the end of the unit you'll be able to write a range of descriptions and structure each one in a way that's appropriate to the purpose and audience of the text. You'll be developing your reading skills too, learning about and practising strategies to help you deal with a text efficiently and critically.

Starter activity

In pairs, decide who is **A** and who is **B**, then follow these steps:
- ★ A: draw a simple shape/pattern on a piece of paper (don't let **B** see it)
- ★ A: describe the shape/pattern to **B**
- ★ B: draw the shape/pattern as **A** describes it
- ★ A and B: compare drawings, then swap roles.

How did you get on? Think about:
- ★ what helped you with your description
- ★ how you structured your description
- ★ what sort of words helped you
- ★ what aspects of your description you could have developed.

Describing an event

read

On 17th April 1986 John McCarthy, a British journalist, was kidnapped in Beirut. Here he describes how his captors prepared him and his fellow captive, Brian Keenan, for a journey they hoped would take them to freedom. Read the extract through carefully twice.

Sayeed had joined the men guarding us. He said that we would be released soon. Then his friends wrapped wide strips of plastic tape around our bodies to keep our arms tight against our sides, and taped our legs together. 'Are we going home?' 'Yes.' They put tape around our blindfolds and then taped pieces of cloth over our mouths. Trussed we were then carried a short distance from the van and pushed into what seemed to be a small metal cabinet. Panic was rising fast within me. But I still clung desperately to the hope that they were tying us up here so that we wouldn't wander away from the designated exchange point…

Once we were moving I had to get more comfortable or risk permanent damage. I wriggled about, managing to loosen the tape around my body. Lying on my back I could now lift my hands and feel the metal sheets that formed the roof of the box. It could only have been eighteen inches high. I worked myself on to my side fearing that in bouncing over rough roads I might smash my face on the panels above. By curling up as far as possible I was able to reach my face, pull down the gag and push up the blindfold.

Feeling a draught on my eyes and being able to gulp in breaths of air eased the panic a little. I'd been terrified that the fumes from the engine would make me vomit and that I'd then choke on it and suffocate. That fear began to fade. I started thinking about the time and number of bolts it had taken to close up the back of the box encasing us. If there were an accident and we drove into a ditch full of water, or the engine caught fire, we wouldn't stand a chance, even if the guards bothered to try to get us out.

Activities

think

1 Read the text again. What are you doing as you read? Are you:
  * ★ picturing the scene (visualizing)?
  * ★ imagining how John McCarthy must be feeling (empathizing)?
  * ★ trying to work out what will happen next (predicting)?
  * ★ asking why the kidnappers need to carry the hostages like this (questioning)?

2 Think about how John McCarthy describes the event. Consider:
   ★ how he describes the way he was taped up (focus on verbs)
   ★ what effect the use of the verb 'trussed' has
   ★ how the writer conveys his sense of panic and hope to the reader
   ★ how the writer manages to make himself slightly more comfortable and how the reader reacts to this
   ★ the sentences used – when does the writer use short simple sentences and what effect do these have?

Checklist

Begin to build up a checklist of some of the features of descriptive writing. How many more features can you add to the list below?

Features of descriptive writing

   ☻ Selective use of powerful verbs help the reader visualize the scene
   ☻ Some personal reflection given
   ☻ Use of first person singular or plural
   ☻ Close details add interest for the reader
   ☻ Range of sentence types used
   ☻ Events described in order as they happened
   ☻ Other features …

Writing

Write a description of an event in your life for a member of your class.

1 Brainstorm the event you are going to describe (e.g. scoring a winning goal, winning a race, starting a new school, etc.). Remember to focus carefully on the detail.

2 Decide how you are going to structure your description. Think about:
   ★ how you are going to open the description
   ★ whether to describe the events in the order that they happened
   ★ which details are going to be essential
   ★ which types of sentences you are going to use
   ★ your choice of verbs and vocabulary.

discuss

3 Write a first draft, then ask a partner for feedback:
★ Is the description of the event clear?
★ Is the level of detail and vocabulary appropriate?
★ Have you used a range of sentences for impact?

4 Produce a final draft, taking your partner's suggestions into account.

Describing a situation

read

The article on page 83 appeared in *The Times* newspaper in February, 2003. It was written by Ellen MacArthur during her race on Kingfisher 2, when she was on a mission to break the Jules Verne record for sailing around the world. Read it through carefully twice.

Glossary

lashing – a cord used to fasten something securely
jury rig – a temporary, makeshift rig
landfall – an arrival at land on a sea journey

think

Activities

1 What are your first reactions to the text?

2 Think about the reading strategies you used. Which did you find most helpful?

3 How does the writer describe the situation? Think about:
★ the sequence of events (starting before the mast breaks)
★ the description of the sound
★ MacArthur's first reactions and later reflections
★ the process of trying to save the mast.

4 How is the piece written? Think about:
★ whether it is in the first person or third person
★ whether it is told in the past or present tense
★ whether the tense changes and, if so, what effect this has.

In a nauseating flash, our challenge is over

WE WERE surfing with the waves doing 20 knots when I was suddenly thrown forward. I heard a gut-wrenching, ear-piercing, crunching and snapping sound.

I was in the navigation station on our 110ft catamaran, Kingfisher2, talking on the satellite phone to our weather router. We were 26 days into our round-the-world record attempt, deep in the southern Indian Ocean. I knew instinctively that it was over.

I dropped the phone and hurled myself towards the companionway, looking round my feet to check if water was coming on board from anywhere: nothing. As I reached the hatch all became clear in a flash of nausea ... the 140ft mast which has powered us ahead of the record over the past 24 days was no more.

My first reaction was to make sure everyone was safe. Fortunately, only the on-watch crew were on deck, (watch leader Neal McDonald, Bruno Dubois, Anthony 'Youngster' Merrington, with Jason Carrington temporarily below) and everyone was OK. We were lucky. If we had been doing a manoeuvre or changing watch systems it could have been different. Then we had to get on with cutting away pieces of the mast and sails that were floating in the water, trying to keep as much as we could.

It took about an hour. We managed to save 10 metres of the mast. Everything else went, including all the sails and rigging. We saw it all float away into the Southern Ocean, along with our chance of breaking the 64-day record.

Most likely we shall never know the cause of our dismasting, and you just have to accept some cases for what they are. These things happen so quickly and no one was looking at the rig the moment before it happened. It was a brand new rig – the guys had worked on it meticulously – and the issues we had in Plymouth (replacing part of the mast-track the day before we sailed) are certainly unrelated.

It would be wrong to say that this trip has not been a massive challenge so far. But equally nothing, at any stage, has brought tears to my eyes. And the tears right now come with the frustration and anger that I feel at having let so many people down.

So much work has gone into this project, so much energy and commitment, each fitting sealed, each lashing tied, and here we were cutting parts of it over the side. It's so destructive, so final.

Sitting here about 2,000 miles west of our new destination, Perth, I feel empty and sad, but above all relieved that no one, bar our boat, was hurt.

At the same time I feel proud; proud of the strength of the crew, proud of their commitment and humour, proud of their smiles and proud of the way they, too, have handled their frustration. The strange thing is that suddenly, although we are all disappointed, we have shifted our focus on getting ourselves moving, and to Australia as soon as we can. With our jury rig we should make landfall in about two weeks.

I glance at my notebook to jot down something and see pages and pages of notes preparing things for this trip. All of a sudden, our challenge feels days away, almost a distant memory. Just three hours ago I was having stitches put in my hand after cutting it open when a rope ripped through it in a manoeuvre. An hour ago I was cutting through rigging as if there was no tomorrow. Now even that seems irrelevant – no longer are we living each day for our 24-hour distance run or thinking about every aspect of boatspeed. Our attempt to break the 64-day record, the Jules Verne, is over.

It's a funny feeling sitting out here thinking about all that has happened, and wondering what might have been. But 'what ifs' will always exist in life. They will never disappear, but you can choose to ignore them ... what's done is done and, however you want to look at it, you learn from it. We must just get up and on to the next challenge.

5 Look at the range of sentences types MacArthur uses. Jot down a few examples. Think about:
★ why this range is important
★ where MacArthur uses short simple sentences
★ what effect these have on her description.

6 Look at the use of verbs in the article. Think about:
★ whether they are powerful/effective
★ what else you notice about them.

checklist

Checklist

Think about the techniques MacArthur uses in her description. How many techniques can you add to the list started for you here?

Techniques to describe a situation

✪ Describe the situation before and after the main event
✪ Include some personal reflection
✪ Use a range of sentences used for effect
✪ Other techniques ...

write

Writing

Describe and reflect on a memorable situation you have found yourself in. Target your writing at someone of your own age. Include as much information as possible to allow the reader to picture the scene. Write two or three paragraphs in total, and remember that detail is very important!

1 Decide on a situation (e.g. being lost, in an exam, at a party).

2 Think about the description:
★ Are you going to use the first or the third person?
★ How are you going to start the description?
★ Where in the description will you need to include close detail?
★ Where and how are you going to include any personal reflection?

discuss

3 Prepare a first draft, then ask a partner for feedback on:
★ the strategies used while reading the piece – did your description make your partner visualize, question, predict, etc.?
★ the vocabulary – is it appropriate to the audience?
★ the range of sentence types, adjectives and verbs used.

> **4** Revise your first draft, bearing in mind your partner's comments.
> Be prepared to share your description with the rest of the class.

Describing a process

read

In pairs, decide on a possible definition of a 'process', then:
* ★ check your definition by looking up the word in a dictionary
* ★ brainstorm as many different types of processes as you can think of.

The text on pages 86-87 comes from a chocolate company's web site. Read it through carefully twice.

discuss

Activities

1 What does the first paragraph do?

2 How do the sub-headings work?

3 Apart from the sub-headings, how else does the writer guide the reader through the description of the chocolate-making process? Think about:
* ★ words that link cause and effect
* ★ temporal connectives.

4 How is the piece written? Think about:
* ★ whether it is written in the first or third person and why
* ★ how formal the writing is and why
* ★ whether it is written in the past or present tense and why

5 Look at the vocabulary used and consider:
* ★ whether there are any words you don't know
* ★ whether the text helps you to work them out.

6 What do notice about the style of the text? Does the writer use adjectives? If so, how and when?

7 This process could be represented as a diagram. Make a few rough sketches of how the diagram might look, then share your ideas. What do you notice? Think about:
* ★ what you have to change
* ★ how you can develop your ideas further.

How is chocolate made?

Chocolate is a sweet treat made from cocoa beans, the fruit of the cacao plant. With its roots firmly found in Mexico, chocolate has been enjoyed for centuries. In America, chocolate manufacturing began in 1765. Beans were shipped in to Massachusetts from the West Indies in the late 1700s, and waterpower was used to grind and prepare beans.

The cacao tree

The cacao tree is a tropical American tree commonly found in wet, lowland areas. Today, cacao trees are found in the Caribbean, Asia, Africa and the South Pacific Islands. Cacao trees are sensitive and cannot be exposed to much sunlight or wind. Therefore, the cacao flourishes in the shade of much taller surrounding trees. Cacao trees rise some 40-feet high and contain 1-foot long leaves. Small, pink flowers dot the leaves and trunk of the tree. Hand-sized pods or fruit hang from various areas of the tree and trunk. Each pod contains 25-50 seeds, which are known as cocoa beans. Mature trees bear 50-70 fruits each year.

Harvesting

Cocoa beans are harvested twice a year. During the harvesting process, the fruit is cut from the tree and split open with a large axe. The beans and pulp are then removed from the pod and placed in holes in the ground or shallow boxes, where they will begin a process of fermenting.

Fermenting

Common grade pulp ferments for a period of 5-7 days, during which time workers frequently turn and mix the beans and pulp. Flavour development begins during the fermentation process. As the beans take on moisture, they expand, turn a brownish-red colour, and take on a sharp fragrance. Once fermenting has finished, beans are sun or kiln dried and bagged. The bags of beans are now shipped to a cleaning factory.

Cleaning

The bagged beans are now subjected to several methods of cleaning to remove contaminants. Twigs, rocks, dust and other debris are separated from the beans. Once cleaned, beans are weighed and blended with different types of beans. Specific mixtures of beans are used when making items such as candy bars, cocoa mix and cocoa butter.

Roasting

Clean beans are roasted to enhance flavour, reduce acidity and lower their moisture content. Roasting also detaches the shell from the bean and deepens the colour. Roasting can last from 30-minutes to 2-hours, depending on the variety of bean.

Winnowing and crushing

During the winnowing process, beans are removed from their thin shells with cracking machines and then separated by means of a high speed fan.

The "nibs" of the bean, which are made of 53-percent cocoa butter are then conveyed to mills, where they will be crushed. Using large grinding stones or steel discs, friction and heat liquefies the cocoa butter and forms chocolate liquor. Liquor is poured into moulds, where it sits until it has hardened.

Distribution

Hardened cakes of chocolate are sold to cocoa manufacturers and factories, where the dark chocolate is then turned into a variety of products including cocoa mixes, eating chocolate, liquors, baking cocoa and more. In the United States, chocolate is most often shipped in liquid form and then processed locally.

Glossary

pulp – soft, fleshy part
kiln – a furnace or oven
contaminant – something that makes another thing impure
debris – scattered pieces of rubbish or remains
winnow – blow a current of air through the shells in order to remove the beans
liquefy – turn to liquid
liquor – a liquid produced in a process of some kind

Checklist

Add as many features as you can to the checklist below.

Features to include when describing a process

- ✪ Sub-headings to highlight specific parts in the process
- ✪ Written in the third person with an appropriate level of formality
- ✪ Use of present tense
- ✪ Connectives to link cause and effect, and to sequence events
- ✪ Other features ...

Writing

Research a process, then produce a description of it for a nine-year-old, e.g.
- ★ How Fruit Juice/a Football is Made
- ★ How Tea/Coffee is Produced

1 Gather together and organize as much information as possible.

2 When you have finished your first draft, ask a partner for feedback:
- ★ Is the process clearly described?
- ★ Is the vocabulary appropriate to the age of the child it is aimed at?
- ★ Are there any technical words that need to be explained?
- ★ Do the diagrams/connectives support the description of process?

3 Prepare a final copy to share with the rest of the class.

Unit plenary

Discuss what you now know about writing descriptions of an event, a situation and a process.

Additional writing tasks

1 **Short writing task.** Write a short description (no more than 150 words) describing how chocolate is made.

2 **Longer writing task.** Write a detailed description of an event or situation where you felt frightened. Encourage your reader to visualize, empathize, etc.

Real Writer: Şenay Camgöz

I'm Şenay and I'm Parliamentary Officer for The National Autistic Society (NAS), the national charity for people with autistic spectrum disorders and their carers. Autism is a disorder that affects the way a person interacts with the world around them and it's my job to make sure that MPs know what it means to live with this disorder.

Before writing to politicians – to ask them to sign a Manifesto, for instance – I decide on the particular problem I want to draw their attention to by discussing the options with my team. For example, the NAS recently did a survey to find out if its members know what benefits are available to them. We analysed the results of this survey and found that many people with autism are still not getting the benefits they are entitled to.

Analysing the results of a survey or any other data is very important as it forms a part of my research and it gives me lots of vital statistics to present to the MPs. There is often a lot of information to get through – so I skim and scan the material until I find the really relevant bits. I always keep the main issue at the front of my mind and try to be really selective, making quick judgements about what's useful and what's not. If I didn't do this, I'd drown in data – there's so much of it out there these days!

Next, I make sure that I have a clear, thorough understanding of the issue we have chosen. After all – if *I* don't understand the problem, how can I make sure the MPs *will*? Then I decide exactly what I want the MPs to do about it before I tackle a first draft.

MPs receive masses of post every day, so it's vital that the briefing grabs their attention and can be read quickly. The aim is to persuade MPs to take action, so the text needs to include a clear analysis of the problem (with statistics to back it up) followed by a logical outline of what they can do to help. It needs to be immediately obvious to the MPs what it is I am asking them to do.

I love my job as it means I get to help give vulnerable members of our society a voice – and that makes a real difference. To those of you who want to make sure even the weakest voice is heard: know your stuff and make it clear and focused!

Objectives

In this unit you will learn how to:
- ✪ weigh different viewpoints and present a balanced analysis of an event or issue
- ✪ undertake independent research using a range of reading strategies, applying your knowledge of how texts and ICT databases are organized and acknowledging sources.

Introduction

Have you ever disagreed with someone about something? If you have, you'll know there are at least two sides to every argument and that it's perfectly possible that each side will think their point of view is the right one.

To be fair to both sides of an argument, you need to look at both viewpoints, examine the issue, then make a fair, balanced judgement … and that's analysis. It's all about breaking a topic down into parts and examining it in detail. Producing a balanced analysis isn't easy, especially if you have strong personal views on an issue, so in this unit you'll be developing your ability to explore such issues in writing that is balanced and thoughtful. By the end of the unit you'll be familiar with the reading and writing strategies needed to create a good, balanced analysis.

Starter activity

With a partner, skim the following comments and sort them into two groups: those you feel are balanced views, and those you feel are one-sided.

A

The government ought to recommend the expulsion of asylum seekers from British soil.

B

Although animal experimentation can be cruel, a careful consideration of the figures suggests that the benefits to human life must be considered before abolishing such research.

C

It is wrong to use animals in scientific experiments.

D

Though I would not send my own children to private schools, I can acknowledge that they may have several features in their favour.

E

On the one hand, asylum seekers are subjected to wrongful discrimination. On the other hand, they can create great problems for the communities in which they placed.

F

Private schools should be abolished.

G

Space exploration is a waste of time and money.

H

Whilst some famous cases have been used to assert that the earth has been visited by extra-terrestrials, many of us are still doubtful about the existence of life on other planets.

discuss

Was there anything about some of the comments above that helped you make the decision quickly? What was it? Share your ideas with the class.

Remember!

Balanced points:
- Offer more than one viewpoint
- Use modal verbs (may, can) to suggest levels of uncertainty

Unbalanced comments:
- Give fixed, single opinions or viewpoints
- Use modal verbs to stress certainty (should, ought)

Facts and opinions

read

The article about immigration on pages 92-93 has been adapted from an item by Steve Schiffers that appeared on the BBC News Online website on Monday 17 June, 2002.

Skim read the whole article. As you do so, make a note of any key features in the text that tell you that the writer wants to offer a balanced view.

think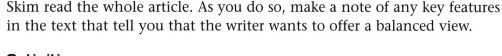

Activities

1 Scan the text again. This time pick out:
- ★ five pieces of useful factual evidence
- ★ five points that are against immigration
- ★ five points that are for immigration.

discuss

2 Share your ideas with a partner, and compile a full list of findings.

3 What do your findings tell you about the writer's sense of balance?

Analysis: Who gains from immigration?

The political controversy over immigration has intensified in Britain and other European countries in recent months, and influenced recent elections in the Netherlands, Denmark and France. Many of those opposed to further immigration fear it may bring in its wake more crime, and some believe that it will jeopardise common values.

But much of the argument about immigration centres around its economic costs and benefits. Opponents say that immigrants are taking the jobs of native workers, and lowering the wages of others. Supporters of immigration argue that it has long-term benefits for the economy, providing needed skills and helping to boost economic growth. And there is a related argument about the costs and benefits of immigration to governments. Do immigrants pay more in taxes than they receive in benefits?

Scale of immigration

The first task in any discussion is to get the scale of the immigration issue in perspective. Immigration has been increasing in the last decade, but its scale is still far smaller than the peak of international migration – in the late 19th century – when some 17% of Europe's working population moved to the New World, mainly to the United States, where 30% of the population was foreign-born by 1910. Immigration into the EU has averaged around 1.4 million each year, compared with some 2.3 million into the United States. And about 5.3% of Europeans are foreign-born, compared with 10.3% in the United States, and nearly 25% in Australia.

What has changed is the spread of countries around the world from which migration now occurs, with Africa and Asia replacing Europe as the main source of immigrants. More people have also entered Europe as asylum seekers in recent years, accounting for around one-third of immigrants – although it has declined sharply from its peak during the Bosnian and Kosovo crises. But more immigrants are also coming as high-skilled workers to take temporary jobs in areas of shortage, such as teaching, nursing, and high-tech computer jobs – and governments are encouraging that trend.

Effect on wages

Some of the biggest controversy among economists concerns the effect of immigrants on wages. Much of the evidence has analysed the effect of Hispanic migration into the United States. The leading scholar on the subject, Harvard professor George Borjas, says that unskilled migrants do lower the wages of native workers who are competing with them for jobs like catering, child-care and cleaning. But this can be offset by the gains made by employers who can make higher profits because of the lower wages. Mr Borjias argues that skilled migrant workers who fill jobs where there are genuine shortages can provide real benefits. In Europe, there are even bigger skill shortages, due to a falling birth rate, and many migrants have higher education levels than Hispanic migrants to the USA.

Most economists believe that the current rise in unemployment has little to do with immigration, and more to do with the high costs of employing new workers, or firing old ones. Unemployment rose rapidly in many EU countries during the 1980s when immigration was stable.

Taxes and benefits

Many immigrant families are larger than average. If this trend continues, this could lead to higher public expenditure, for example on education. However, most immigrants are of working age, which means they consume less of the services provided by the state, such as health care and education, and pay more in taxes. In the UK, Home Office research suggests that immigrants pay £2.5bn more in taxes than they take in benefits.

Moreover, the main demographic problem facing Europe is a declining birth rate, which is threatening to make it difficult to pay for pensions for future generations. Some commentators have suggested that increased immigration could offset the growing pension burden on a smaller workforce. The EU has rejected this argument, however. It says that the numbers of projected immigrants would not be enough to overcome the lack of people of working age, and other measures are necessary, such as increasing the participation of older workers and women in the workforce.

Long term growth

In the long term, the addition of more people to the workforce should boost economic growth. Evidence from economic historian Nick Crafts, of the London School of Economics, suggests that the huge migration from Europe to America in the late 19th century did boost the growth rate in the US, and contributed to its economic take-off. But the key to that growth was a huge, open internal market. It is this single market that the EU is still in the process of creating. If it becomes a success, then the economic problems of immigration are not likely to loom large in the future.

Glossary

controversy – disagreement on a matter of opinion
Bosnia and Kosovo – Eastern European site of civil war and ethnic cleansing
Hispanic – from or of Spain or Spanish-speaking countries,
EU – the European Union
demographic – statistics of birth, death, disease

4 Look at the section 'Scale of immigration' again, this time more closely. Think about:
★ what important facts it adds to the discussion
★ how this factual material helps to support the analysis as a whole.

5 Scan the whole article. How does the writer back up the facts and opinions he presents with evidence?

The structure of analysis

think

Activity

Now look at the structure of 'Analysis: Who gains from immigration?'. You may find it helpful to draw a rough diagram of the layout of the article, blocking out the space taken up by the headings, text, etc.

How is the analysis structured? Think about:
★ the introduction – what is the purpose of this introduction? How can you tell from the introduction that the writer intends to give a balanced analysis, rather than a one-sided argument?
★ how the sub-headings guide the reader through the article – skim read two sub-sections to gather evidence
★ how the writer divides up the ideas into paragraphs under each sub-heading – check one sub-section for evidence
★ how the writer concludes the analysis in the final section.

Remember!

✪ An introduction outlines the topic.
✪ Sub-headings – which are not always used in analysis – indicate the topic of each section; sub-headings can be replaced by topic sentences.
✪ Each paragraph deals with a separate point, which is explored in some detail; sometimes two sides of that point are examined.
✪ The conclusion summarizes and can also look forward to the future by commenting on what might happen next.

write

Writing

You are now going to write the introduction and two topic sentences for an analysis on asylum seeking. Asylum is linked to immigration because a proportion of immigrants to the UK come seeking asylum from their own country, sometimes because of war, famine or other human rights issues.

As preparation look at the facts and opinions below. They are the type of facts and opinions you might find if you researched the topic on the Internet. Decide:
★ which points you think are negative
★ which points are definitely fact
★ how you might match up the points to make balanced statements.

All asylum seekers are 'bogus scroungers' who take advantage of UK charity.

Asylum seekers with no official papers cannot return to their country of origin.

The rising number of refugees has become an issue across Europe.

Research by homeless charity, Shelter, has found that one in six of the dwellings provided by local authorities for refugees are unfit for human habitation.

75,000 people claimed asylum in the UK in the year 2000.

At most, asylum seekers get aid and cash and kind amounting to 70% of the minimum income support offered to UK citizens.

Most asylum seekers come from the poorest most war-torn places – Somalia, Iraq, Iran and Sri Lanka.

Asylum seekers should be kept in detention centres and then returned to their country of origin.

Economic migration helps to fill labour market shortages, improve public finance, and contribute to the development of industries and jobs.

Use your notes to help you write:
★ the introduction to an analysis on asylum seeking
★ topic sentences for two paragraphs of this analysis.
You may add words and phrases of your own if you wish.

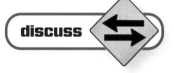

discuss

Discuss your first draft with a partner. How did you decide what to include?

The language of analysis

You are now going to look at the article on pages 92-93 from a different angle – at the language that the writer uses. The language used is, like the structure, very important to the overall success of a piece of analysis.

think

Activities

1 Reread the first section of the article (up to the first sub-heading). Look at the second sentence in the article and decide:
★ what the two reasons for opposing further immigration are
★ how the writer signposts these reasons as points of view, not facts.

2 Look at the second paragraph of the article. Which connective tells us that the writer has another view to express?

3 In this opening section how has the writer made sure that his readers:
★ consider several viewpoints?
★ keep an open mind?
★ will read on?

4 Reread the section 'Taxes and benefits'. How has the writer balanced the ideas in each paragraph? Pick out points for and against immigration.

5 Which words signpost the way the writer balances opinions?

6 Which words suggest the writer has an open mind and wants to keep a tone of uncertainty?

7 Now look at the final section. Pick out the verbs or verb phrases used in this conclusion, and identify:
★ which tenses are used
★ whether they suggest the present is certain
★ whether they suggest the future is certain.

8 Which words in the last sentence suggest a final sense of balance? Do you think that this is a satisfactory conclusion? Why? Why not?

Remember!

- Viewpoints are balanced with well-chosen connectives (and, but, however).
- Sentence structure is balanced ('many of those ... and some believe ...').
- Neutral language is used (some, many, supporters, opponents).
- Subordinate clauses are used to express reservation and contrast.
- Several points of view are presented with equal weight.
- Modal verbs express a degree of uncertainty.
- Questions are used to make the reader contribute to the thinking process and want to read on.
- Words like 'if', 'some', 'could' and 'suggested' allow for uncertainty and different opinion.
- Each paragraph considers two viewpoints.

Writing

Write one paragraph of an analysis on asylum, plus a short conclusion.
★ Use as much of the material on page 97 as you can.
★ Focus on making the paragraph balanced and well expressed.
★ You may make grammatical changes (modal verbs, for example).
★ Use contrasting or comparative connectives.

Share your work with a partner. How have you managed? Is your expression clear? Are your ideas balanced?

Separating myth from reality is not easy, but the idea of the scrounging, bogus asylum seeker, is among the common misconceptions.

At most, asylum seekers get aid and cash and kind amounting to 70% of the minimum income support offered to UK citizens.

Some councils are left seriously out of pocket as a result of the influx of asylum seekers.

Research by homeless charity, Shelter, has found that one in six of the dwellings provided by local authorities for refugees are unfit for human habitation.

Refugee aid groups and even police have expressed concern that negative media reports are leading to racist attacks on refugees housed in deprived areas.

write

Writing

Write your own balanced analysis of a controversial topic. Choose one of the topics below, or agree a topic of your choice with your teacher.

★ The issue of asylum seeking
★ Using animals in medical research
★ Charging motorists to enter big cities
★ Paying enormous sums of money for footballers on transfer
★ Teenagers having television in their bedrooms

1 Decide on a controversial topic.

2 Do some research to get a factual basis for your analysis. The Internet is an excellent starting point, but remember that many web sites exist to support a particular cause, and may be biased! You need a range of different sources to balance your ideas.

3 Plan your work. This will help you to balance the different opinions and include useful factual background on the topic.

4 Structure your analysis. Match up opposing points, so that you can build paragraphs round the contrast or comparison of similar points. Decide on the order of your points.

5 Decide how you are going to present the analysis, e.g. as a web page, newspaper article, etc. Think about its layout and appearance.

6 Draft your introduction, outlining the topic. Then draft the main paragraphs. Use formal language and balance the views. Use the checklists in this unit to remind yourself of features to include.

7 Choose a suitable title for your analysis.

8 Share your first draft with a partner. Ask for feedback on the following:
★ Is the topic clearly outlined in the introduction?
★ Have a range of points been chosen?
★ Are the ideas clearly and logically organized in paragraphs?
★ Is the analysis balanced?
★ Is the language of analysis used (see checklist on page 96)?

9 Prepare a final draft of your analysis, taking any feedback into account.

Unit plenary

Share your achievements in writing analysis.
★ What are the challenges of writing this text type?
★ What aspects of analysis will you need to practise in the future?
★ In what other subjects might you be asked to do this sort of writing?

Additional writing tasks

1 **Short writing task**. Teachers and students have mixed views about examinations and testing. Write a short, balanced analysis of testing for publication in a school newsletter.

2 **Longer writing task**. Under proposed laws police, teachers and education authority staff will be allowed to issue fixed penalties of £40 to £60 to truants, vandals or troublemakers. Write a balanced analysis of this proposal.

Real Writer: Yehuda Sinai

Hi there! My name is Yehuda and I'm a senior engineering consultant in a company that develops specialized engineering and scientific software. My part of the company deals with calculating the movement of liquids and gases, for example:

★ Flow of air around aeroplanes, cars and trains.
★ Flow and cooling of chocolate during manufacturing.

My job also involves selling our consultancy services and helping our sales staff to sell the software. This means I often need to make oral presentations to a range of audiences, from just a handful of people to larger audiences of several hundred at a conference.

The first task is to decide on the basic message of the speech or presentation with my colleagues. This often means persuading the audience that the work we have done for them is good enough, that our software does the job and is cost-effective, or that the science behind some calculations is of good quality. If the persuasion works, we get paid!

Then, once I know *what* to say, I have to work out *how* I'm going to say it. The structure of the speech is the easy bit, as it normally involves an introduction, a main, middle part and, finally, a conclusion. It's the wording that's trickier. Here, it's absolutely vital to keep the audience in mind. My subject is generally very technical, so if I present it in great detail to people without a scientific background, they'll either be blinded by the science or bored stiff. On the other hand, a highly qualified specialist may become irritated – or even insulted – if the presentation is too simplistic. The challenge gets even harder when I'm faced (as I usually am) with the most difficult audience of all: a mixture of specialists and non-specialists. Luckily, I enjoy the challenge!

Humour can be a great icebreaker and I often use it in my speeches. If used appropriately, it can really help to break down any barriers but again it's important to consider the audience. We don't all have the same sense of humour!

So now you know about the persuasive speeches I have to make and how I go about making them. You also know *why* I need to make them – that's how I help the company to survive! All that's left to add is how much I enjoy the variety being a scientist and engineer brings – as you can see, it's not just science, it's English skills too! Speaking of which, can you identify the introduction, main part, and conclusion on this page?

Objectives

In this unit you will learn how to:
- ✪ present a case persuasively, making selective use of evidence, using appropriate rhetorical devices and anticipating responses and objections.

Introduction

If you wanted to become the Prime Minister, how would you get people to vote for you? One way would be to make a persuasive speech, telling your voters exactly why you would be the best person for the job.

Most speeches are written down before they are delivered. They are powerful texts designed to persuade their audience to do or believe something. They use rhetorical devices – language techniques that have a persuasive or impressive effect on an audience. Editorials – newspaper or magazine articles written by the editor – use many of the same techniques to put forward a persuasive viewpoint.

In this unit you will explore a range of editorials and speeches, identifying key rhetorical devices before writing your own pieces of persuasive text.

Starter activity

Think of a situation where you had to persuade someone to do or agree with something. What kind of arguments did you use to persuade them? Jot down some ideas. Be prepared to share your thoughts with the class.

In pairs, read the following extracts and decide which ones you think are persuasive and which ones are not.

A

Anyone who uses the public libraries knows that they are obsessed with computerization. Where once you had a neat card index in a polished mahogany nest of filing cabinets, you now have an electronic slum of sprawled printouts and scattered microfiches. Doubtless the computer is enormously useful to librarians wishing to check that the book they have not got is equally unavailable in other branches, but I don't see why it has to be inflicted on the customer. The fact is that most electronic gadgetry is the enemy of literature ...

B

Come on now, ladies and gentlemen, who will start the bidding? I hear 12.4 per cent over there in Kent. Any advance on 12.4? Who will give me 15 per cent? Yes, you, sir, well done, 16 per cent. And do I hear 20 per cent? My goodness, a forest of hands for 20 per cent. Can anybody do better than a 20 per cent increase in their council tax this year?

C

I started writing poems when I was about 18 years old. I had wanted to be an artist and thought that I would try using words instead of pictures. As for Reluctant Writers – well, don't worry about it. If you're not keen that's OK. Some kids aren't sports-mad; that's OK too. You need to be able to write for some purposes, but you don't need to be a Writer.

D

At 8.15 on Friday night, Sukhjit Chhoker and his girlfriend Melinda Smith were gazing through the viewfinder of their camcorder at the illuminated façade of Barcelona's Gothic cathedral. Suddenly, a well-dressed man appeared and began speaking loudly at them in Spanish, gesticulating wildly. The pair tried to explain that they did not understand – but they soon would. As the man spoke, his two accomplices swiftly relieved them of their backpack and made off into the night. Sukhjit gave chase, following the three men to a nearby metro station.

think

Activities

1 How did you know whether the extracts above were persuasive or not? What helped you make a decision?

2 Try reading the extracts aloud. Does this help you to decide? If so, why?

3 Focus on the persuasive texts. What techniques have the writers used to put their ideas forward persuasively? Think about:
★ the tone
★ the choice of words
★ the sentence structure
★ rhetorical techniques (language techniques that have a persuasive or impressive effect on an audience) – e.g. repetition, appeal to the reader, emotive language, etc.

Checklist

Begin a checklist of persuasive techniques. How many techniques can you add to the list started for you below?

Persuasive techniques

- ✪ Rhetorical questions (questions that do not require an answer as they are designed to persuade)
- ✪ Use of the second person to appeal directly to the reader
- ✪ Use of supporting evidence, e.g. facts and figures
- ✪ Use of poetic language such as imagery and alliteration to make points colourful and memorable
- ✪ Powerful adjectives and verbs
- ✪ Appeal to the reader
- ✪ Emotive vocabulary (words that appeal to the emotions, e.g. words with strong associations such as religion, patriotism, etc.)
- ✪ Other techniques ...

Editorials

read

Below is the opening of an editorial written by Boris Johnson in response to the rises in Council Tax in 2003. Boris Johnson is editor of *The Spectator* and MP for Henley. Read it through carefully twice.

They're bleeding us dry to buy mountains of red tape

Come on now, ladies and gentlemen, who will start the bidding? I hear 12.4 per cent over there in Kent. Any advance on 12.4? Who will give me 15 per cent? Yes, you, sir, well done, 16 per cent. And do I hear 20 per cent? My goodness, a forest of hands for 20 per cent. Can anybody do better than a 20 per cent increase in their council tax this year?

Going, going – what was that? Say that again. You cannot be serious. I have here a gentleman who has been asked to find 27 per cent more in council tax this year! He is my friend, the guard at the Palace of Westminster, who watches the members' entrance for forthcoming retaliation by the agents of Saddam Hussein, and I have no reason to doubt him.

His house has not grown in size; his output of rubbish has not increased; nor is his car doing appreciably more damage to the roads this year than last. And yet he has no choice but to cough up a further £400 per year out of taxed income. Add that to his dues under the congestion charge (more than a grand), and the rise in his National Insurance contributions and you are looking at a tax squeeze of Healeyesque viciousness.

The pips are squeaking across the country this April; and this time it is not the rich who are feeling the wrath of the People's Party. It is all of us. Every householder in the land - and particularly the southern parts of the land – is about to pay wildly over the odds to a Blair government which promised not to raise taxes.

It is diabolical, and yet to listen to Blair yesterday you'd think it was nothing to do with him. The rises in council tax are in fact a cynical dodge, and Blair's central government is almost entirely to blame.

Glossary

forthcoming retaliation – return attack about to happen
appreciably – significantly
Healeyesque – Denis Healey was appointed Chancellor of the Exchequer for Harold Wilson's Labour Party in 1974. He imposed tight monetary controls including deep cuts in public spending.
wrath – extreme anger
to pay over the odds – to pay more than what is generally considered acceptable
cynical – distrustful

think

Activities

1 Who is the intended audience for this piece?

2 What is the intended purpose of this text? Think about what the writer is arguing against.

3 Look at the title. Think about:
   ★ what its purpose is
   ★ how effective you think it is.

4 How does the writer start the piece? Think about:
   ★ what effect this has on the reader
   ★ the effect of this piece if it is read aloud.

5 Think about the use of questions and answers. What effect do they have?

6 Look at the sentences the writer uses. Think about:
   ★ whether they are simple, compound or complex
   ★ what effect these have on the reader.

7 Look at the third paragraph. How does the writer develop his argument at this point?

8 What persuasive techniques does the writer use? Think about:
   ★ the opening paragraph
   ★ the writer's language choices
   ★ emotional appeal.

9 Look at the writer's use of evidence to support his point of view. How does he put his evidence forward?

10 Think carefully about the writer's reference to his friend. Why do you think he includes this?

write

Writing

Imagine you are the editor of your school newspaper. Write an editorial using the following information about proposed changes to the school year.

Should there be a six-term school year?

The school calendar in England could be transformed into a six-term year, with shorter holidays and earlier exams.

The Independent Commission's controversial proposals could end the hayfever misery of high summer exams.

It could also mean A-level students could apply to university after their exams already knowing their grades.

There are also proposals for summer holidays to be staggered in different regions.

The government says it has no plans to back a change and stressed parents, teachers and school governors would have to agree with the Local Government Association's proposals.

The current school year was devised more than 100 years ago – so shouldn't we keep something that has worked for so long? Or is this the change parents, children and teachers have been waiting for?

Adapted from BBC News Online

1 Before you start writing, think carefully about:
* ★ what your point of view is
* ★ how you are going to present your point of view persuasively
* ★ the techniques you are going to use (look back at the checklist on page 100 to remind yourself of persuasive techniques)
* ★ how you are going to begin your piece (remember how important it is to catch your reader's attention).

2 Consider the structure you are going to use. How are you going to develop your ideas through the editorial? Think carefully about your paragraphs. How are you going to link them? What effect will each sentence have on the reader?

3 Write a first draft of your editorial.

discuss

4 Swap your first draft with a partner and ask:
* ★ Is it written in the right tone for the intended audience?
* ★ Is it clear?
* ★ Does it follow a structure?
* ★ What are the best bits?
* ★ How persuasive is it? Which rhetorical devices are used?
* ★ Are there any weaker bits? If so, how could they be developed?
* ★ Is the vocabulary appropriate?
* ★ Are the sentence types varied for effect?

5 Revise your editorial, taking on board the feedback you have received.

6 Proof-read your work before you prepare and present a final version.

Speeches

Speeches, like editorials, are used to persuade people to a particular point of view. They are also used to support or challenge the listener. The speech in this unit is in written form, however the way in which a speech is delivered is very important and something you need to bear in mind. A good delivery helps to make a speech persuasive and memorable. The speaker's tone of voice, the pauses, eye contact, and facial expression are all powerful aspects of giving a speech.

The extracts below are taken from the speech made by John F. Kennedy in his Inaugural address (the first speech he made as President) in Washington, D.C., January 20, 1961. At this time there was a state of political hostility known as the Cold War, which existed between the alliance of Soviet countries and the Western powers. The Cold War began after WW1 and was characterized by political threats, violent propaganda and other activities, but never involved open combat. It ended in 1990.

Read through each extract carefully twice. (Keep an eye out for some US spellings!)

1

We observe today not a victory of party but a celebration of freedom, symbolizing an end as well as a beginning, signifying renewal as well as change. For I have sworn before you and Almighty God the same solemn oath our forebears prescribed nearly a century and three-quarters ago. The world is very different now, for man holds in his mortal hand the power to abolish all forms of human poverty and all forms of human life. And yet the same revolutionary beliefs for which our forebears fought are still at issue around the globe, the belief that the rights of man come not from the generosity of the state but from the hand of God. We dare not forget today that we are the heirs of that first revolution.

Let the word go forth from this time and place, to friend and foe alike, that the torch has been passed to a new generation of Americans, born in this century, tempered by war, disciplined by a hard and bitter peace, proud of our ancient heritage, and unwilling to witness or permit the slow undoing of these human rights to which this nation has always been committed, and to which we are committed today, at home and around the world.

Let every nation know, whether it wishes us well or ill, that we shall pay any price, bear any burden, meet any hardship, support any friend, oppose any foe, to assure the survival and the success of liberty. This much we pledge – and more.

Glossary

forebears – ancestors

to abolish – formally to put an end to something

at issue – under discussion; in dispute

tempered – made resilient

2

Let both sides explore what problems unite us instead of belaboring those problems which divide us. Let both sides, for the first time, formulate serious and precise proposals for the inspection and control of arms and bring the absolute power to destroy other nations under the absolute control of all nations. Let both sides seek to invoke the wonders of science instead of its terrors. Together let us explore the stars, conquer the deserts, eradicate disease, tap the ocean depths and encourage the arts and commerce. Let both sides unite to heed in all corners of the earth the command of Isaiah to 'undo the heavy burdens (and) let the oppressed go free' …

In your hands, my fellow citizens, more than mine, will rest the final success or failure of our course. Since this country was founded, each generation of Americans has been summoned to give testimony to its national loyalty. The graves of young Americans who answered the call to service surround the globe. Now the trumpet summons us again … a call to bear the burden of a long twilight struggle … against the common enemies of man: tyranny, poverty, disease, and war itself.

Can we forge against these enemies a grand and global alliance, North and South, East and West, that can assure a more fruitful life for all mankind? Will you join in that historic effort? [Crowd shouts approval]

In the long history of the world, only a few generations have been granted the role of defending freedom in its hour of maximum danger; I do not shrink from this responsibility – I welcome it. The energy, the faith, the devotion which we bring to this endeavor will light our country and all who serve it …

And so, my fellow Americans – ask not what your country can do for you, ask what you can do for your country. My fellow citizens of the world – ask not what America will do for you, but what together we can do for the Freedom of Man.

Finally, whether you are citizens of America or citizens of the world, ask of us here the same high standards of strength and sacrifice which we ask of you. With a good conscience our only sure reward, with history the final judge of our deeds, let us go forth to lead the land we love, asking His blessing and His help, but knowing that here on earth God's work must truly be our own.

Glossary

to belabor – to argue in excessive detail
to invoke – to call on
to eradicate – to destroy completely
to tap – to exploit
commerce – buying and selling
to heed (… the command) – to pay attention to
course – route or direction
to forge – to create

think

Activities

1 What is Kennedy setting out to do in this speech? Think about:
   ★ why he is making the speech
   ★ what you know about the politics of the time (you may want to do some research here).

2 Who do you think his audience was? Who is the 'we' Kennedy refers to?

3 Why did this speech need to be so powerful?

4 Look at the first sentence of extract 1. Think about:
★ how Kennedy opens the speech
★ what effect the use of 'we' rather than 'I' has
★ why he then moves on to using the first person.

5 Look at the way Kennedy starts each sentence in the first paragraph of extract 2. What effect does this have?

6 How does Kennedy persuade his audience? Think about:
★ the effect of the rhetorical questions
★ his appeal to the audience's emotions, religious beliefs, sense of patriotism, etc.

7 What does the crowd's response show?

8 How does Kennedy conclude his speech? How effective is this?

Checklist

Make a checklist of persuasive techniques used in speeches. If you wish use the list below as a starting point. How many techniques can you add?

Persuasive techniques in speeches

- Powerful opening and conclusion
- Repetition of key words and phrases
- Rhetorical questions
- Uniting the audience and the speaker
- Connectives to link ideas
- Sentences that build to a climax
- Use of 'if' to start a point
- Lists used for emphasis
- A range of sentence structures for effect (e.g. short, powerful statements)
- A persuasive tone
- An appeal to the audience's emotions, sense of loyalty, patriotism, faith, etc.
- Use of first person to add a personal appeal
- Use of exaggeration, humour, play on words, etc.
- Use of shock tactics (surprise or horrify the audience)
- Make personal views come across as common sense
- Other techniques ...

Writing

write

You have just been elected to one of the following positions. Write a short speech about what you intend to do when you are in that role.

★ Head boy or girl
★ President of a local group, e.g. an animal rights group
★ Captain of the local football/netball team
★ Leader of a local sports club

1 Choose a role. Think carefully about:
  ★ the purpose of your speech (to persuade your audience to do/believe/support something) and the subject matter
  ★ the intended audience.

2 Think about how you are going to structure your speech.
  ★ How are you going to present your ideas?
  ★ How are you going to develop your points?

3 Think about what sorts of persuasive devices you are going to use. (Remind yourself of the devices listed in the checklists throughout this unit.)

4 Think about the evidence you could use to support your case. Will it be specific, general, or will you use a combination of the two?

5 Decide how you are going to start your speech.

6 Write a first draft.

discuss

7 Read your speech to a partner. Ask for feedback on the following:
  ★ Is your purpose clear?
  ★ Have you developed the points persuasively?
  ★ Have you used a range of persuasive techniques?
  ★ Does the opening of the speech grab the listener's attention?
  ★ Is the ending effective? Does it pull all the relevant points together and end with a key point?

8 Redraft and proof-read your work, taking into account all the feedback you have received. Remember to check the spelling, punctuation and content of your writing.

Activity

Speeches are intended to be delivered orally (spoken) to an audience. Prepare to give your speech to the class. Practise in small groups first to work on your delivery.

Remember!

⭐ Look around you as you speak so that every member of the audience feels that you are talking to them.
⭐ Pause when you want to make a specific new point.
⭐ Vary your tone of voice: lower your voice to underline a specific point or raise it to get attention.
⭐ Think about how facial expressions can support your point of view.
⭐ What sort of gestures might you use to make a point?
⭐ Think about body language. How are you going to stand?

Unit plenary

Discuss:
★ what you have learnt about editorials and speeches
★ what aspects of persuasive rhetoric you want to develop in your work
★ what aspects you found harder to work on and why you think that was
★ how what you have learnt can be applied in other subject areas.

Additional writing tasks

1 **Short writing task.** You have been asked to write short piece for your local newspaper about a proposed skateboard park on the outskirts of a residential area. You feel very strongly that this project should go ahead, but you know there are many local residents who are against the idea. Persuade your readers that the project should go ahead.

2 **Longer writing task.** You have been chosen to represent the school in a speech-making competition. Write a speech on a subject you feel very strongly about. Persuade your audience to your point of view.

Real Writer: Jane Ramsey

Hello, I'm Jane Ramsey and I'm a copywriter for Oxfam, an international charity working to end world poverty. I'm lucky to have a really varied job, which ranges from writing speeches for popstars at Glastonbury festival, to producing fundraising adverts for the national press, to creating promotional materials for Oxfam shops.

One of the most challenging parts of my job is to persuade people to get involved in campaigns to make the world a fairer place. This often involves explaining quite complex issues, such as global trade rules or Third World debt, in a very clear way. It's not just about informing people though – it's about making them realize they have the power to change things, and inspiring and persuading them to take action.

Whether I'm writing a 1000 word feature or a 100 word email, the key thing is to grab people's attention from the word go, perhaps with a shocking fact or a powerful quote. I make sure I know who the target audience is, and use language which is appropriate for them. Then I develop the argument in a logical way, always backing up statements with evidence and examples. It's really important to show the impact an issue or situation has on real people – I use quotes where I can: a plea from a mother who can't feed her children is much more powerful than several paragraphs explaining a famine. Say what you mean, and don't be tempted to use more words than you really need!

I do research too, which often involves looking up information on the Internet, talking to other staff, and looking for good photos and case studies. When I have a good understanding of the subject, I write a first draft, but I usually have to redraft it a few times before everyone's happy with it.

It's a fantastic feeling to know that thousands of people could read what I've written – and better still, that, as a result, some of them will be inspired to act on it. So, if you feel passionate about something, don't keep it to yourself – *get writing*!

Objectives

In this unit you will learn how to:

✪ develop and signpost arguments in ways that make the logic clear to the reader

✪ integrate evidence into writing to support analysis or conclusions, e.g. data, quotation.

Introduction

Have you ever struggled to express your opinion clearly or found it difficult to persuade other people to see your viewpoint? This unit aims to develop the skills you need to present an argument logically, in writing, using evidence to support your point of view.

As well as learning how to present a clear argument, this unit also focuses on discursive texts – texts in which you try to look at different sides of an issue, and weigh up which is most valid, usually in the conclusion.

Activities

1 Brainstorm the following questions, jotting down your ideas:

★ Where might you find argument texts?

★ What is their purpose?

2 Make a list or mind-map of all the things that you would expect to find in an argument text, for example:

- The writer's opinion expressed clearly, at the beginning of the text
- Evidence to support the opinion
- Text written in the first person for a personal effect

Presenting an argument

read

Read the extract below. It is taken from an article on the BBC web site about Prince Charles' views on children's reading and their use of computer games.

Prince battles video games

The Prince of Wales has called for lottery money to be used to tempt children back to books, theatre and the arts – and away from their computer games.

'One of the great battles we face today is to persuade our children away from the computer games towards what can only be described as worthwhile books,' he said.

Prince Charles spoke of the need to 'expand the minds and fire the imagination' of children.

'None of us can underestimate the importance of books in an age dominated by the computer screen and the constant wish for immediate gratification,' he added.

The prince was speaking at a reception hosted by the Millennium Commission at the British Museum in London to recognize a project that distributes literary classics to school libraries.

From www.news.bbc.co.uk/1/hi/technology/1433290.stm *Wednesday, 11 July, 2001*

think

Activities

1 What does Prince Charles want to tempt children back to?

2 How does he describe this?

3 What does he feel children want from computer games?

4 What is the role of the Millennium Commission?

5 Why do you think he made this speech at the British Museum?

read

Overleaf are some responses to Prince Charles' views. Read them carefully.

1

'I wholeheartedly agree with Prince Charles but I am more optimistic than him.

There was such a huge emphasis on computer screens and going online over the last decade. But more and more people agree that there is no point in having extraordinarily fast ways to communicate if there is nothing really valuable to say.

I think it has become very apparent that children would be losing something valuable by not reading but I feel more cheerful because book funds are going up.

Studies show that schools which emphasize books have better results and children who read more have a better understanding of themselves and of the world they live in.'

Anne Fine, author of children's novels

2

'Computer gaming is a hugely satisfying pastime, that takes a valid place amongst other forms of entertainment.

Contrary to popular misconceptions there is no credible psychological evidence that shows that video gaming is anything but beneficial, but there is evidence that supports it as having educational benefits and further that it is a social pastime.

Playstation is a much more compelling form of entertainment because it is interactive. It isn't passive entertainment, players can take control of a story and change the outcome, players can participate in their favourite sport and score that winning goal, or lift that championship cup.

Books are an excellent form of entertainment but provide different stimuli and are extremely meritorious in their own right – but I see the two sitting side by side rather than conflicting with each other.

I suppose like all things in life, there is a question of moderation. If people choose a balance, then each form of entertainment is valid, beneficial and satisfying.'

David Wilson, Sony Computer Entertainment Europe

3

'Reading and computer games both have a part to play.

Often the criticism of computer games stems from ignorance. Parents in their 30s who grew up with computer games now see their children playing them – it is natural for them.

'Parents of Prince Charles' generation have a fear factor because it is not natural for them.

Books have been around for centuries but if they came into our lives today and children went off to their bedrooms to be on their own for hours reading – would we be that happy?

Computer games also have educational benefits – they improve hand/eye co-ordination, but also a lot of games require children to think strategically and to plan, which are skills which can be taken into the classroom.

There is also such a broad variety of computer games and they are not all about shooting or killing people. The most popular game in the UK in 2000 was Who Wants to be a Millionaire?'

Mike Rawlinson, general manager of the European Leisure Software Publishers' Association

From www.news.bbc.co.uk/1/hi/technology/1433290.stm
Wednesday, 11 July, 2001

think

Activities

1 Decide whether each writer is arguing for or against Prince Charles' point of view.

2 Look carefully at how each writer develops his or her argument. Copy and complete the grid below to record your analysis.

Analysis	Extract 1	Extract 2	Extract 3
Name and job of writer			
Devices used to develop argument, e.g. names of specific games, statistics, research.			
How is the argument concluded? Which is most effective and why?			
Are simple, compound or complex sentences used?			

discuss

3 Discuss your findings with a partner. Then, together, draw up a list of techniques used by writers to put forward effective arguments. Your list may begin something like this:

Techniques for effective arguments

- ✪ Use of first person to emphasize a personal point of view
- ✪ Reference to the other person's argument
- ✪ Use of research to support an argument
- ✪ Specific examples used to support a point of view
- ✪ Use of connectives to signal a difference in argument, e.g. 'but', 'contrary to', 'on the other hand', 'for example'
- ✪ Other techniques ...

Writing

You are now going to have a go at writing your own piece to argue either in favour or against Prince Charles' point of view. Follow the steps below.

1 Think about how you might respond to Prince Charles' views.

2 Decide how you are going to introduce your point of view.

3 Think about how to develop it – refer to your checklist for ideas.

4 Draft your opening sentences, choosing words carefully for the greatest effect. Then draft the rest of the piece.

5 Share your work with your partner. Check whether:
★ you have stated your opinion clearly at the outset
★ you have signposted your ideas effectively
★ you have used connectives to develop your argument
★ you have used evidence/research to support your point of view
★ you have concluded your piece effectively.

6 Revise your work carefully bearing in mind your partner's feedback. Proof-read it thoroughly to check spellings, grammar and punctuation.

Discursive texts

You are now going to explore how a writer can look at arguments both for and against an issue. This type of text is often referred to as a 'discursive text'.

Read the discursive text on the next page.

Video games: Cause for concern?

Huge hype surrounds the launch of each new games console – the Sony Playstation 2 is just the latest. But should parents be worried by their children's passion for virtual play?

Foremost among the criticisms levelled at video games is that they are addictive. The charge goes that they can lead to compulsive behaviour, loss of interest in other activities, association mainly with other addicts, and unusual symptoms when addicts are denied their favourite pastime – such as the shakes. Sound familiar?

A decade ago research showed that video game junkies were highly intelligent, motivated and achievement-oriented individuals. They did well at school and work. But could the more sophisticated games of the 21st century be so all-consuming as to interfere with that kind of achievement?

Dr Mark Griffiths of Nottingham Trent University, an expert on video game addiction, thinks it could just happen. 'The video games of the 21st Century may in some ways be more psychologically rewarding than the 1980s games in that they require more complex skills, improved dexterity, and feature socially relevant topics and better graphics. If these games offer greater 'psychological rewards', players might be more at risk of developing an addiction,' he said.

Children are drawn to video games at about the age of seven. For most, the games remain a harmless activity, but a small minority could be termed 'addicts'. A recent study of children in their early teens found that almost a third played video games daily, and that – more worryingly – 7% played for at least 30 hours a week.

Dr Griffiths is concerned by that figure. He said: 'What are the long-term effects of any activity that takes up 30 hours of leisure time a week on the educational, health and social development of children and adolescents?' Such dependency could feed other delinquent behaviour such as stealing money to buy new games, truancy, failing to do homework, or simply extreme annoyance when unable to play.

One symptom of over-exposure which parents might pick up on is stiffness in their children's movements. With 40% of family homes now containing computers, there is plenty of opportunity for children to get to a screen. But most terminals are set up for parents, and the children are the ones who make do.

The resulting bad posture is one of the chief causes of repetitive strain injury (RSI) among children, according to Bunny Martin, director of the Body Action Campaign, a charity trying to combat the disorder among young people. She says children as young as seven are suffering from RSI because of overuse of computers at school and in the home.

In some classes of 11-year-olds, she has found that more than half the pupils have the first signs of the condition. A 13-year-old-boy from Peckham, south west London, told her: 'At night my thumbs are so painful I have to sit with them in cold water to take the pain away.'

A constant criticism levelled against video games has been that the majority feature aggressive elements. This in turn has been used to argue that children become more aggressive as a result of playing them.

The controversy has raged for 15 years, but little systematic research has been carried out, and the debate becomes increasingly relevant as new games use more explicit representations of extreme and realistic violence. The theory of social learning says that playing aggressive video games leads to the stimulation of aggressive behaviour.

On the other hand, the catharsis theory suggests that playing aggressive video games has a relaxing effect by channelling and releasing aggression.

Dr Griffiths says that while more research is needed, it now seems clear a child's play after watching a violent video game becomes more aggressive. 'It is probably the case that violent video games have a more pronounced effect in young children but less of an effect – if any – once they have reached their teenage years,' he added.

This extract is adapted from the web site www.news.bbc.co.uk/1/hi/uk/1036088.stm

think

Activities

1 What is the purpose of the text?

2 How does the writer present the arguments?

3 What effect do the questions in the text have?

4 Copy and complete the table below, using information from the text.

Arguments for computer games	Arguments against computer games
1. '10 years ago research showed that video game junkies were highly intelligent, motivated and achievement-orientated individuals' 2. 'For most, the games remain a harmless activity'	1. 'They are addictive'

5 Look at the type of sentences that the writer uses. Are they simple, compound, complex or a combination?

6 How does the writer use evidence to develop the arguments?

7 Look at the topic sentences used by the writer. What effect do they have? (Remember that topic sentences are near the beginning of a paragraph and signal what the rest of the paragraph is about.)

8 How has the writer achieved cohesion through the text? Look carefully at the use of connectives, e.g. 'foremost', 'on the other hand'.

9 What can you conclude from the final paragraph? What is Dr Griffiths' opinion?

checklist

Checklist

Draw up a list of features that you have identified in the above text. Your list might start like this:

Features of discursive texts

⭐ Rhetorical questions used to introduce the arguments
⭐ Evidence used to support a particular point of view
⭐ Connectives used to develop a point of view, e.g. 'Foremost'
⭐ Connectives used to contrast a point of view, e.g. 'On the other hand'
⭐ Use of quotes from experts
⭐ Range of sentence types
⭐ Writer sometimes presents his or her opinion on the subject as well
⭐ Other features ...

write

Writing

Write your own paragraph to replace the final one in the text above. Give your opinion about whether video games are a cause for concern. Remember you will need to refer to some of the key arguments in the piece as well as giving your own opinion. Follow the steps below.

> **1** Think carefully about how you are going to start the piece, e.g. 'In conclusion...', 'Having explored the evidence...', 'Personally...'.

discuss

> **2** Draft your conclusion and then share it with a partner. Ask them:
> ★ Is the beginning of the paragraph effective?
> ★ Is there evidence to support the opinion?
> ★ Are connectives used to develop the argument?
> ★ Is the final sentence effective?
> ★ Is there variety in the sentence structure?

> **3** Revise your work, taking account of your partner's suggestions. Proof-read for errors in grammar, punctuation and spelling.

Writing your own discursive text

write

In this unit you have explored texts that present one side of an argument and texts that explore two sides of an argument. Write a discursive text about mobile phones entitled 'Mobile phones – a cause for concern?'

Preparation

Read the following two extracts for ideas that you could include in your text.

1

Mobile phones cut schoolgirl smoking?

Mobile phones could be a surprise weapon in the health education campaign to cut smoking among young women.

Doctors attending a conference this week in London heard 'anecdotal evidence' that the upsurge of use of mobile phones among teenage girls was slowing the rate of increase in smoking.

There has been much concern among health education officials over the growing numbers of teenage girls who are taking up smoking.

But there were suggestions at a conference organized by the British Thoracic Society and the University of East London's Centre for Public Health Policy that mobile phones could be taking the place of cigarettes as a way of making schoolgirls feel grown-up.

Status symbols

'Image is most important in the taking up of smoking and one of the attractions for young girls is that it makes them feel adult,' says William MacNee, Professor of Respiratory and Environmental Medicine at the University of Edinburgh.

'And the speculation is that the mobile phone could play a similar role in making them feel adult, lessening the need for cigarettes.

'Mobile phones could be filling a gap in the growing up process that has sometimes been taken by smoking.

'Being seen to have a mobile phone is an important sign of entering the adult world – and as with smoking there is much peer pressure associated with it,' said Professor MacNee.

Although this remains as only a theory, Professor MacNee draws parallels between the way teenagers use phones and the rituals of smoking – with both serving a social and display purpose.

'You see young people holding a phone, as though they're about to use it – it's something in their hand – and there are similarities to the rituals of smoking,' he says.

From www.news.bbc.co.uk *Friday, 6 October, 2000*

2

Using a mobile gives driver 'tunnel vision'

Drivers who talk on a mobile at the wheel suffer from a lethal form of tunnel vision – even if the phone is hands free.

Scientists have discovered that talking on a mobile causes 'inattention blindness' which slows reaction time and cuts drivers' awareness of their surroundings by up to half.

The researchers warned that mobile users who believe that they are driving safely because they have a hands-free kit are fooling themselves as it is the conversation that is distracting rather than the way in which it is conducted.

Mobile phones have been implicated in at least 19 fatal crashes in Britain since 1988 and the latest research is likely to increase calls for a wider ban on using a mobile at the wheel.

A law coming into force at Easter will impose fines on users – but drivers with built-in hands-free units will be exempt.

Researchers monitored the reaction times, monitoring style and performance of 110 men and women driving 40 miles in a simulator. Talking on a hands-free phone reduced the amount of visual information they processed by about 50 per cent...

Drivers took longer to brake and to accelerate while talking on the hands-free phone. All of the accidents recorded during the study happened when people were talking on a phone.

The researchers then used an eye tracking device to find out where subjects were looking while using the simulator. They discovered that, while the drivers looked at the objects around them – including road signs, other vehicles and traffic lights – as they drove, they could not remember seeing them if they were talking on the phone.

From an article by Tim Utton, Science Reporter,
The Daily Mail, January 30, 2003

Planning

1 Research other arguments for and against mobile phones. Gather evidence you can use to validate the arguments. Think about cost, how mobiles can keep people in touch, etc. Make a list of points.

2 Think carefully about:
   ★ how you will begin your **introduction** e.g. There are arguments both for and against the use of mobile phones …
   ★ how you will introduce the **arguments** – are you going to organize your paragraphs into arguments and counter-arguments?
   ★ how you will use evidence/data/experts to **develop your arguments**
   ★ how you are going to **connect your ideas**
   ★ what type of **sentences** you are going to use?

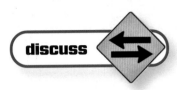
Evaluation

Share your first draft with a partner. Ask him or her to identify the strengths and areas for development. Check that:
★ the arguments are set out clearly
★ evidence is used to back up the arguments
★ connectives are used to link ideas and guide the reader through the text
★ a variety of sentence structures is used
★ the conclusion expresses a clear opinion.

Unit plenary

Discuss what you have learned about texts that argue a point of view and discursive texts. Create a graphic prompt to remind you of the structure of each type of text, using boxes, bullets and lines.

Additional writing tasks

1 **Short writing task.** Write a piece of text, no more than 250 words, arguing either for or against one of the following:
★ school uniform
★ fox hunting.

2 **Longer writing task.** Research and write a discursive text entitled: 'Fox-hunting: yes or no?'

Real Writer: Naomi Bracegirdle

Hi! I'm Naomi, a dentist working in general practice. To treat a patient successfully, I need to build his or her trust in me. That way, he or she is more likely to undergo treatment and to listen to my advice.

The most common advice I find myself giving is: how to eat healthily; how to keep teeth clean; what to do following certain treatments, such as extractions and fillings; and advice on the various treatment options a patient has. To make sure the advice I give is clear and easy to understand, I follow a few key points:

Give advice in writing – I always back up any advice I give with a leaflet that covers everything I have said. The careful structure of the leaflets – which can include headings, sub-headings, short, clear sentences, lists of DOs and DON'Ts, bullet points and illustrations – make the information easy to read, take in and remember.

Give advice in the right manner – I make myself approachable by speaking calmly and in a friendly way. I don't use complicated language, and adapt the language I do use to suit the individual patient. When giving instructions I sometimes need to be quite firm, but I always make sure 'being firm' doesn't turn into 'being bossy' – otherwise the patients would run a mile and my advice would fall on deaf ears!

Use visual aids – Making use of visual aids can make my advice clearer by giving it a practical context. An example of this would be demonstrating to a patient how to clean his or her teeth properly using a toothbrush as a prop.

Beware of information overload! – I make sure all the advice I give is relevant and to-the-point so as not to overwhelm the patient.

Rewards and results – These are really important. I might reward a child who has followed my advice with a sticker, or by praising their efforts. For older patients, the rewards are often the results themselves – such as healthy gums if they've been cleaning their teeth well!

My job is great as it means I get to meet people from all walks of life. I haven't got bored with it yet, and don't think I ever will! My advice? If you're thinking about becoming a dentist, go for it!

Objective

In this unit you will learn how to:

⭐ give written advice which offers alternatives and takes account of the possible consequences, e.g. money management for young people.

Introduction

We are all presented with occasions, throughout our lives, when we give or accept advice from others. We might find ourselves advising friends or family members, even offering advice to a complete stranger (as an employee in a bank or travel agency, for example), or be on the receiving end of someone else's advice, such as parents or teachers. Sometimes advice can be just as hard to give as it can be to accept!

This unit aims to develop the skills you will need to be able to read and then write your own advice texts, focusing on how to offer alternatives. You will explore a range of advice texts, looking at how they are constructed and then use the knowledge you gain to write your own texts.

Advice texts provide the reader with information to help them. They can be written for a range of slightly different purposes and audiences, but fundamentally they are written to advise people. This means they may contain aspects of other text types too, e.g. they may be persuasive or instructional.

Starter activity

With a partner, jot down all the things that you already know about advice texts. You may find it helpful to organize your ideas into a mind-map like the one below.

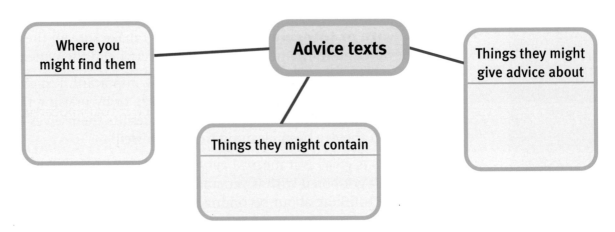

Where you might find them

Advice texts

Things they might give advice about

Things they might contain

discuss

Activity

In small groups of four or five, discuss what advice you would give in the situations below.

★ Jot down the advice you would give.
★ Be prepared to explain the advice to another group/pair.
★ Have you given suggestions or instructions, or both?
★ Have you given alternative suggestions or just one?

A

My younger brother is always scribbling on my school work and I then get into trouble at school.

B

I want to take up a new hobby but I am not sure how to go about it.

C

I want to stay over at my friend's house next weekend, but my parents are not very keen.

D

I want to get a part time job but I am not sure if I am old enough or how to go about it.

E

I have not been selected for the school football team ... again. What can I do about it?

Giving personal advice

read

The text on page 126 is a response to a letter that appeared on the BBC web site. Read it through carefully twice.

Ask the Doctor

Q: Eating before exercise

My daughter is on the school netball team – they often have a match straight after school but she is starving after lessons and has asked me to pack a snack tea for her. Can she eat before exercise or will it give her cramps?

Meg

Dr Trisha Macnair responds

Because of the dire warnings which used to be put about regarding eating before swimming, and the risks of drowning because of muscle cramps, many people are very wary about eating before any exercise. But if the exercise is only moderate and you're not thinking about a 3 course meal, it's very unlikely to lead to problems.

Food before action can help

In fact many top-class athletes do better when they have snacked before, or even during exercise (think of all those tennis players shown in the middle of long Wimbledon matches scoffing bananas!).

If you eat before getting into action, especially if it is hours since lunch, at the end of a long school day, food will restore and maintain blood sugar levels. If your daughter doesn't snack she is more likely to feel weak, faint and tired during the game. Her brain performance will be affected too, so she will be less quick off the mark, and less able to judge ball speeds or decide what tactic to play. Performance all round is worse, so the right sort of snack may help her win, by sustaining her energy and improving her ability to play well! It will certainly mean she enjoys the game more.

Some people feel worse for food

A few people find that eating before exercise actually makes them feel worse, with indigestion or sleepiness – you can only learn by personal experience.

During moderately paced activity (such as the stop-start action of netball) the body is able to carry on digesting food and the chances of nausea or discomfort after eating is much less. But with more intensive sports, such as aerobics or running, the blood supply to the gut is reduced in order to send blood to the muscles instead. In this case the food is much more slowly digested, so it is more important not to eat (especially a large meal) for several hours before action.

Good pre-sport snacks

Carbohydrates are the key – they provide energy in an accessible form to maintain blood sugar and glycogen levels, and are easily digested. Try some of the following, ideally about 30 minutes before exercise:

- Cereal bars
- Sandwich
- Bananas
- Muffins
- Raisins
- Fruit juice

Glossary

carbohydrates – e.g. sugars and starch; can be broken down in the body to release energy

glycogen – a substance deposited in bodily tissues as a store of carbohydrates

Adapted from the website http://www.bbc.co.uk/health/ask_doctor/eating_before_exercise.shtml 8 December 2000

think

Activities

1 What is the purpose of the text?

2 Who is the intended audience?

3 How is the text structured? Think carefully about:
★ the question   ★ the use of sub-headings
★ the opening   ★ the bulleted list.

4 How is the text written? Think about whether:
★ the text is formal or informal
★ the reader is directly addressed
★ the writer uses a variety of sentence structures, e.g. are they simple, complex or compound, or a mix?

5 Look at the sub-heading 'Some people feel worse for food'. Think about:
★ what effect this has on the reader
★ what the doctor is doing here.

6 Find examples of the following in the text:
★ modal verbs
★ conditional sentences
★ connectives.
Why has the writer used them, i.e. what job are they doing?

checklist

Checklist

Draw up a checklist of possible features of personal advice texts, looking back through the work you have done in this unit so far to remind yourself. You may choose to begin your list like the one below.

Features of personal advice texts

- ✪ Written in response to question
- ✪ Written directly to the person who asked the question but accessible to anyone
- ✪ Use of sub-headings to identify key points
- ✪ Reader often directly addressed, e.g. 'you'
- ✪ Conditionals used to signal how something depends on something else, e.g. 'if you eat before getting ...'
- ✪ Modal verbs used to signal possibility/alternatives, e.g. '... so the right sort of snack may help her win'.
- ✪ Other features ...

write

Writing

Now try out the skills you have learned so far by writing a short piece of advice. Respond to the following question, written to an 'agony aunt' called Sue.

> Dear Sue,
>
> Shortly I will be moving with my parents to a new area. I will have to go to a new school and I am worried that I will find it hard to make friends. Please can you advise me what to do?
>
> Anne, 12

Remember that you need to respond to Anne's concerns, while also making the advice applicable to anyone else who may find themselves in a similar situation. Think about:

★ the audience – who are they?
★ the tone that you are going to use
★ the vocabulary that is going to suit your audience
★ how you are going to start your response
★ how you are going to develop your advice – are you going to use sub-headings and/or bullet points?
★ how you are going to offer a range of alternatives
★ how you are going to conclude the piece.

discuss

When you have finished drafting your work, check your own writing and then review it with a partner. Talk about how you made the decisions about organization, vocabulary and sentence structures for this particular target audience. Be prepared to share your responses with the whole class.

Giving general advice

read

The text below is from the NSPCC web site. Read it carefully twice.

Adapted from the website
http://www.nspcc.org.uk/homepage
2/campaign/safe_surfing.htm

Advice on surfing safely

Chat rooms and messaging can be great fun, but remember, you never really know who you are talking to online. It could be someone trying to trick you, some kind of weirdo, or someone really dangerous.

To make sure you are safe:

- **Never use your real name** in chat rooms – pick a special online nickname.
- **Never ever tell anyone personal things about yourself or your family** – like your address or telephone number, or the school or clubs you go to. That goes for sending them photos as well (that way if you don't want to hear from them again, you only have to log off.) Remember, even if somebody tells you about themselves, **never** tell them things about you.

If you arrange to meet up with someone you've only spoken to online, remember that they **might not** be **who** they said they were, so **only meet people in public places and take along an adult** – they should do this too, because they don't know who you really are either!

Never respond to nasty or rude messages, and never send any either! If you feel suspicious or uncomfortable about the way a conversation is going, or if it's getting really personal, save a record of it and stop the conversation there and then. That way you can show someone and ask what they think.

Be careful with any email attachments or links that people send you, they might contain nasty images, or computer 'viruses' that could ruin your PC. So if you don't know who it's from, definitely don't open it.

Avoid sites that are meant for adults. You might be curious, but sometimes these sites can be difficult to get out of, they can cost more on the phone bill, and they can detect your email address and start sending you stuff you really don't want to get. And if you see rude pictures where they shouldn't be, always let an adult know so they can get them removed.

Agree some rules with your parents or carers about what you can and can't do on the Net. It'll save arguments later. You probably know more about using it than they do, though, so make sure they know what they're agreeing to!

Don't let it take over your life! Keep up your other interests and try and use the Internet with friends and family, not just on your own.

think

Activities

1 What is the purpose of this text?

2 Who do you think this is aimed at? Who is the audience?

3 How is the text structured? Think about:
★ the way the subject is introduced
★ how the text is developed
★ the effect the bold font has
★ the effect the bullet points have.

4 How is the text written? Consider:
★ whether it is formal or informal
★ whether or not the writer uses a variety of sentence structures
★ how the writer is addressed – what effect does this have?

5 How does the writer 'command' the reader? Think about:
★ the use of imperative verbs and the effect this has on the reader
★ the use of exclamation marks.

6 In the text, the writer frequently offers the reader a variety of alternatives. How does the writer do this? Which word is used to signal that an alternative is about to be given?

checklist

Checklist

Look through the following checklist of features of general advice texts. How many more features can you add?

Features of general advice texts

- ✪ Often directly address the reader, e.g. 'you'
- ✪ Use a variety of presentational devices for effect
- ✪ Use of imperative verbs to give instructions
- ✪ Vocabulary and tone suitable to the target audience
- ✪ Other features ...

write

Writing

Using the knowledge of advice texts that you have gained so far, produce an advice sheet on revising for exams, aimed at Year 8 and Year 9 pupils. Design your sheet so that it could be used as a page on your school's web site. You might like to use the information on page 131 as a starting point.

DO start revising well before the exams to give yourself more time to absorb the information.

DO take short breaks at regular intervals – get some fresh air, have something to eat/drink.

DO begin your revision gently as much as several months in advance, then build it up as the exams draw near.

DON'T try to tackle everything at once – divide your revision up into bite-size pieces.

DO ask your teachers for advice on how to focus your revision.

DON'T revise when you're tired as you won't take anything in – have a proper rest, a good night's sleep, then try again.

DO revise in a group – two heads can be better than one and you can bounce ideas off one another.

1 Think about:
- ★ what points you want to make
- ★ how you are going to attract your readers' attention
- ★ if and how you are going to use illustrations/pictures/cartoons
- ★ layout (remember it's for a web site!)
- ★ how you will organize your ideas.

2 Draw up some plans for your advice sheet. Consider:
- ★ your audience
- ★ what sort of tone you are going to use
- ★ whether your advice sheet is going to be formal or informal.

3 Remember to refer back to the checklists in this unit! Think about:
- ★ offering alternatives
- ★ the use of modals, conditionals and connectives.

4 Now write a first draft.

Swap your work with a partner and check his or her advice sheet against the features on the checklists. Think about and discuss the following points:
★ Is it written in an appropriate style?
★ Is the advice clearly set out and easy to follow?
★ Which features are used effectively?
★ Suggest two areas that could be developed further.

Think carefully about the feedback from your partner, then edit your work to produce a final copy of your advice sheet.

Unit plenary

Discuss:
★ what you now know about advice texts – share your ideas as a class, thinking about the range of advice texts that you have explored through this unit
★ points you can now add to your original mind-map.

Additional writing tasks

1 **Short writing task.** You are the 'counsellor' for the school magazine. You receive the following letter asking for advice. Write your answer.

> Dear John,
>
> I am really worried about a couple of girls in my year group. They often make silly comments and jokes about me. I have tried to ignore them but they still do it. What can I do?
>
> Sian, 13

2 **Longer writing task.** Research and write a leaflet giving pupils advice about what to do if they are bullied. You will need to make sure that you have researched the subject thoroughly and that you handle the advice in a sensitive and thoughtful way.

Real Writer: Dan Curley

Hello! I'm Dan and I'm Deputy Editor of *The Official PlayStation Magazine*, where I spend a considerable amount of my time editing the reviews section. This involves sourcing all games to be reviewed, planning the page space for each game, then deciding who writes what.

Some reviews I write myself, others I send out to freelance writers. Finding the best person to write the review is half the task. Many *PlayStation* games require a specialist opinion and if, say, a football management simulation comes in for review, it's essential that the person who reviews it knows that field of gaming inside out.

The best reviewers are able to fuse fact with opinion from start to finish. Simply writing 200 words of fact followed by 100 words of opinion is no good. Your opening sentence has to be captivating and injecting humour into the opening is a great way to achieve this. From then on, facts about the game content and personal opinion need to be woven together into an entertaining read. Don't just say what's in the game, say what's in that warrants your opinion, be it positive or negative.

It's also essential that the flavour of the game comes across. How does it feel to play? What are its special features? Can the Hulk punch through walls? Can you play as Inter Milan? Can Mario do a triple somersault? It's the details that make the review; the number of levels and weapons you can leave for the back of the box. Pick a level and describe what you do in it. Choose a weapon and describe what happens when you use it on a bunch of zombies!

Always judge each game on its own merit and avoid phrases such as 'fans of the genre will like this more' or 'if you like X, then you'll love Y', which don't tell you anything! Tell your reader if a game is any good or not, and *why*. That's what they want to know, so that's what you need to give them!

Game reviewing is a great job! In fact, sometimes I can't quite believe it *is* a job. Playing games, then writing about them for tens of thousands of people – I can't think of a more fun way to earn a crust this side of space-travel!

Objectives

In this unit you will learn how to:
- ✪ write a critical review of a substantial text, taking account of the context in which it was written and the likely impact on its intended readers.

Introduction

Have you ever read a review that has changed your mind about whether or not to read a book? What was it about that review that got you thinking? Was it the way the reviewer presented his or her opinion of the text in question? Or perhaps it was what the reviewer actually said about the text. What influenced you the most?

A critical review of a substantial text, such as a novel or a work of non-fiction, often puts across the personal opinion of the reviewer. This means that the review will make a judgement – either positive or negative – about the text. In this unit you'll be looking at how a critical review is written, exploring in detail how the text is structured, taking into account the audience and then using this knowledge to write your own critical review. You'll be looking at reviews of novels, but don't forget that the same strategies apply to reviews of non-fiction texts too!

Starter activity

Think about a text that you have read recently. Briefly review it orally for a partner, then discuss what you included.

In pairs brainstorm some of the things you might expect to find in a critical review. Remember that 'critical' doesn't just mean 'negative' – it involves judging, weighing up the pros and cons and arriving at a judgement that can be positive or negative.

Written reviews usually include:

- ✪ information about the title and the author
- ✪ brief synopsis of the plot/subject
- ✪ information about characters where appropriate
- ✪ information about how the text is written (whether it makes the reader want to keep on reading, etc.)
- ✪ suggestions as to who might enjoy the text.

Opening a review

read

Read the following review of Alan Gibbons's latest novel, *Caught in the Crossfire*. The review is by Gillian Cross.

Hatred strolls in by the back door

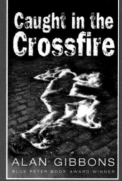

Gillian Cross on Alan Gibbons's suspenseful tale of the evils of racism, Caught in the Crossfire

Saturday April 12, 2003
The Guardian

Caught in the Crossfire
by Alan Gibbons
296pp, Orion, £4.99

[1] Alan Gibbons has made no bones about his reason for writing this book. 'I wanted to explore head-on the conditions in which racism is re-emerging,' he said in a recent article for the *Times Educational Supplement*. *Caught in the Crossfire* is concerned specifically with modern Britain. It encourages readers to look critically at the society in which we live and the complicated ways in which individual behaviour interacts with economic and social pressures.

[2] The book opens with a scene in which Rabia, a Muslim teenager, is harassed on her way home from the library. Simultaneously, a fascist leader from London is driving up the motorway, listening to Lohengrin as he plans his meeting with the local branch of the Patriotic League in Oakfield, the town where Rabia lives.

[3] These two incidents lead into a fast, intricate narrative that cuts skilfully from one group of people to another. Creed, the manipulative fascist leader, finds himself working with a collection of young louts headed by a middle-aged thug who dreams of Nazism. Prompted by Creed, these naive recruits succeed in stirring up enough trouble to provoke retaliation from a group of hot-headed young Muslims – including Rabia's brother, Tahir. While this is going on, Rabia begins to fall in love with a boy called Mike Kelly whose brother (inevitably) joins the Patriotic League.

[4] Gibbons's purpose, as he makes clear on the very first page, is to show that: 'Hatred can be ordinary and evil can be commonplace. They have a way of strolling in by the back door.' He wants to demonstrate how the evil of racist violence strolls into Oakfield, and he does that by presenting an intricate network of causes. It is the details that are crucial in this story. They range from world events, such as the September 11 attacks, to economic and social changes, like the closure of the mill (where people from different local communities worked side by side), and individual actions, including the harassment of Rabia.

⁵Creed and his allies capitalise on existing tensions in Oakfield as they campaign for seats on the local council. The presentation of the town is coherent and convincing, in spite of the occasional blunder (how does Creed, who lives in London, manage to stand as a candidate for election to Oakfield council?), and Gibbons handles his large cast of characters skilfully. The story rattles along, building up suspense and complexity without ever becoming confusing.

⁶Gibbons does not neglect personal relationships (both Mike's family and Rabia's are carefully described), but he is not really interested in what makes people racist. Mike's brother, Liam, joins the Patriotic League because he feels inferior to Mike – but any other organisation that gave him a sense of belonging might have done just as well. Creed is a cardboard villain and so is Stone, the thug with Nazi dreams. What really engages Gibbons's interest is the town of Oakfield itself and the threat to community that is posed by the Patriotic League.

⁷That threat is what gives the book its real impetus. Unlike Malorie Blackman's *Noughts and Crosses*, which is set in a fictional country and challenges its readers to look at their own attitudes and behaviour, *Caught in the Crossfire* looks outwards. It encourages people to think about society and the issues that threaten it. Gibbons lacks Blackman's flamboyance and emotional engagement, but he writes with passionate conviction about the importance of community and the need for ordinary people to resist attempts to destroy it. The most convincing character in the book is the town of Oakfield itself.

Activities

 think

Focus on the opening of Gillian Cross's review. Reread paragraphs 1 and 2 carefully twice.

1 Why do you think the review starts with a heading ('Hatred strolls in by the back door')?

2 Why do you think the information about the title, author and publisher is included at the beginning of the review?

3 How does Gillian Cross open her review? What effect does this have?

4 What is your first impression of Cross's opinion of the novel? Think about:
   ★ whether Cross gives an opinion at the opening of the review at all
   ★ how clear Cross's opinion is.

5 How does Cross go on to introduce the novel? Think about how much information she gives the reader.

6 What is the purpose of the second paragraph?

7 What sort of sentences does Cross use? Is this important?

8 How is the review written? Think about:
   ★ whether Cross writes in first or third person
   ★ whether she uses past or present tense
   ★ whether the tense changes through the review and, if so, why.

9 Who is the intended audience of this review?

Checklist

Begin a checklist of ways to open a review. How many points can you add to the list started for you below?

Ways to open a review

- ✪ Use the title to sum up the text
- ✪ Include information about the title, author, publisher, price, number of pages, etc.
- ✪ Use the introductory paragraph to include a comment on text by its author
- ✪ Briefly touch on the themes of the text
- ✪ Other ...

The text below is from the opening of Adèle Geras's review of *Inventing Elliot*, a novel by Graham Gardner. Read it through carefully twice.

There's an awful lot of glitter and razzle-dazzle around in children's books these days. Epic struggles with bad magic of every variety take up metres of shelf-space. Those volumes have covers heavy with gilded, bronzed or silvered lettering and are full of special effects. This first novel couldn't be more different. It comes dressed in a rather austere greenish dustjacket, but it packs a real punch, partly because it is based on the personal experience of the writer. However, Gardner hasn't just blurted out all the dreadful things that happened to him at school, but has worked the material with great care into a moving and subtle story.

    Elliot is about to start attending Holminster High after having been bullied at his previous school. His mother is at work all day, struggling to keep the family together and solvent. Her husband has been the victim of a brutal attack and now, having lost his job, does nothing but sit at home all day, a shadow of the man he used to be.

think

Activities

1 What is your initial impression of the review? Think about:
   ★ whether the reviewer thinks it is a good novel
   ★ what provides you with this information.

2 How does Geras open her review? Are there any similarities here to Cross's review on page 135–136?

3 Identify any other techniques Geras uses to introduce her review. (Add these to the checklist you started above.)

write

Writing

Write the introduction to a review of a novel or non-fiction text you have read recently. The review should be aimed at young people and adults.

1 Gather the following information:
   ★ title, author, publisher
   ★ key quotes (from the author about the text, from other reviewers, from the text itself)
   ★ main themes
   ★ intended audience
   ★ adjectives to describe the characters, plot, setting, writer's style, etc.

2 Think about how you are going to introduce your review:
   ★ Are you going to include a quote from the author about the novel?
   ★ Are you going to make a comparison with another novel/other novels?
   ★ How are you going to give a brief overview of the main themes?
   ★ Are you going to give your opinion early on and, if so, how?

3 Write a first draft.

discuss

4 Share your work with a partner and ask for feedback:
   ★ How have you opened the review? Is this effective?
   ★ How have you introduced the plot and/or themes? Does this provide the reader with enough information without giving everything away?
   ★ Have you kept the narrative viewpoint consistent, e.g. third person?
   ★ Have you used a variety of sentences? Are these effective?
   ★ Have you given your opinion? How have you introduced it?

5 Revise your first draft taking the feedback into account.

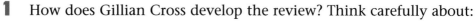

Developing a review

read

Reread paragraphs 3, 4, 5 and 6 of the review on pages 135–136 carefully twice.

Activities

think

1 How does Gillian Cross develop the review? Think carefully about:
- ★ the reference to incidents identified in the second opening paragraph (see page 135)
- ★ the use of a quote from the novel and what this achieves
- ★ the use of adjectives and adverbs to describe the narrative, the setting, characters, etc.

2 What is the reviewer's opinion of the book?

3 How does Cross present her opinion here? Think about:
- ★ the use of adjectives
- ★ the use of adverbs.

4 How does the reviewer signal that there are events that happen simultaneously in the novel?

5 How does the reviewer signal that there is an element in the novel that could be developed further?

checklist

Checklist

Make a checklist of ways to develop a review. You may like to use the following list as a starting point. How many points can you add?

Ways to develop a review

- ✪ Include a relevant quote from the novel (to highlight a key theme)
- ✪ Use powerful adjectives/adverbs (to identify key points) and to convey a very vivid description of the text
- ✪ Use the third person
- ✪ Make clear links between paragraphs
- ✪ Use a variety of sentences for impact
- ✪ Other …

write

Writing

Develop the review you began on page 138. Write two or three paragraphs to form the middle section of your review.

1 Brainstorm the following points:
   ★ How you are going to develop your opinion?
   ★ How you are going to provide your reader with additional information without giving away the entire plot?
   ★ Which adjectives/adverbs are you going to use?
   ★ How are you going to describe the work of the novelist?
   ★ How are you going to signal the area/areas of the novel that could be developed further?
   ★ How are you going to describe the writer's use of characters, setting, etc.?

2 Write a first draft of the middle section of your review.

discuss

3 Share your work with a partner and ask for feedback:
   ★ the way you have linked your paragraphs/ideas to the opening of your review
   ★ how you have described the plot, characters, setting, etc.
   ★ how you have presented your opinion
   ★ whether you have used a variety of sentences
   ★ how you have explored the way the writer deals with the themes/subject matter of the novel.
   Ask your partner to identify three strengths of your work and two areas that you could develop further.

4 Prepare a revised draft taking the feedback into account.

Concluding a review

think

Reread the concluding paragraph of Gillian Cross's review carefully twice (paragraph 7, page 136).

Activities

1 How does Cross connect the final paragraph with the previous one (in the middle section, see page 136)?

2 What impression do you get of the reviewer's opinion in this paragraph?

3 How does the reviewer present her opinion?

4 What do you think about the final sentence? Why do you think the reviewer chose to end her review like this?

read

The following extract is the conclusion of Adèle Geras's review of *Inventing Elliot*. Read it through carefully twice.

> From the press release that accompanies the novel we learn that Gardner is one of 10 children. Elliot (the main character in the novel) is spectacularly on his own, so perhaps the writer's own circumstances weren't quite as bleak as the fictional ones he's set up. Speaking to Louise (a character in the novel) about books, Elliot says: '… they're not just words … when you're reading, you're exploring, reaching out, knowing other people, sharing their lives, everything that happens to them'.
> The world of this particular book isn't exactly idyllic, but it's a pleasure to share it none the less.

think

Activities

1 How does Geras conclude her review?

2 What effect does Geras's use of the quote have?

3 What effect does this final paragraph have?

4 What do you think the reviewer's opinion of the novel is?

Checklist

Start a checklist of ways to conclude a review. If you wish you may use the list below as a starting point. See how many points you can add.

Ways to conclude a review

- ✪ Refer to the way another writer has tackled a similar theme
- ✪ Include some personal opinion
- ✪ Use a relevant quote from the novel
- ✪ Use a strong final sentence
- ✪ Other ...

Reread the whole review of *Caught in the Crossfire* carefully twice.

Activity

In pairs, discuss how the reviewer has:

- ★ developed her opinion
- ★ linked the paragraphs together
- ★ maintained the use of the third person
- ★ used a variety of sentences.

Writing

Write the conclusion to your review. Remind yourself of the opening and middle sections you prepared earlier in this unit.

1 Think carefully about:
   - ★ how you are going to tie the review together
   - ★ whether you are going to use a quote
   - ★ what impact your final sentence is going to have.

2 Write a first draft of your conclusion.

3 When you have finished drafting your conclusion, go back to your opening and middle sections. Read your whole review through carefully. Are there any changes that you want to make? Think about:
★ whether you have provided the reader with an overview of the plot
★ whether you have presented your opinion clearly and developed it throughout the review
★ whether you have linked your paragraphs effectively
★ whether you have used a variety of sentence types
★ whether the ending of your review is effective.

discuss

4 Show your work to a partner. Ask for feedback on:
★ any area you need to develop further
★ anything you need to make clearer
★ how you could improve your review.

5 Prepare a revised draft, taking account of your partner's suggestions.

Unit plenary

discuss

Discuss:
★ what you have learnt about writing reviews
★ what you found particularly effective when writing your review
★ what aspects of review writing you need to work on further.

Additional writing tasks

write

1 **Short writing task.** Write the opening paragraphs of a review of a text you have read recently. If you have already written a review of a novel in this unit, then choose a non-fiction text to review now. Similarly, if you have already worked on a review of a non-fiction text, this is your chance to tackle a review of a novel. Write no more than 200 words.

2 **Longer writing task.** Write a full review of a novel or a non-fiction text that you have read recently. Refer back to the checklists in this unit to remind yourself of ways to write a successful review.